SHORT LESSONS *in*
WORLD HISTORY

Third Revised Edition

E. Richard Churchill
Linda R. Churchill

J. WESTON
WALCH
PUBLISHER

Portland, Maine

Photos on the following pages appear courtesy of
AP/WIDE WORLD Photos:

118, 133, 139, 147, 148, 155, 160, 162, 165, 168, 173, 174, 175

Photos and art on the following pages appear courtesy of
Dover Pubications:

7, 12, 64, 68, 69, 72, 74, 82, 83, 89, 95, 96, 105, 106, 108, 112, 114

1   2   3   4   5   6   7   8   9   10
ISBN 0-8251-3941-4

CONTENTS

INTRODUCTION

This latest edition of *Short Lessons in World History,* like its predecessors, presents the fascinating story of human history in a concise form. It combines ease of reading with subjects of high interest.

This edition retains the best of previous editions. It begins with an introductory section on maps, a section that helps learners understand the location of the events they are tracing. In addition, each unit contains a brief biography of an outstanding historical figure.

But this edition has more. It concludes with the startling world events and global power blocs that have shaped the 1990's. This edition also challenges students with new critical-thinking questions called "Think About It."

Short Lessons in World History was originally written by Linda and Dick Churchill for presentation to their own Colorado students. Those students liked the book, as have thousands of others. We know that thousands of additional students will now begin to appreciate this new revision. We hope that you are among that group, and that this book will lead you to a greater appreciation of the exciting, complex world in which we live.

MAPS HELP US UNDERSTAND WORLD HISTORY

Introduction

The history of our civilization takes us back many years. Learning about world history takes us far from our own nation. When we study something that happened long ago and far away, we need special tools to help us learn.

Maps are one of the most useful tools in the study of world history. They give us a picture of where events took place. By using a map, we can get a good idea of where nations are or were located.

Finding Locations on the Map

Our earth is a huge *sphere*, or ball. About one fourth of the surface of the earth is covered by land. Water covers the other three fourths of the earth.

Sometimes we use a *globe*, which is a model of the earth, when we want to see where a city or nation is located. At other times we use *maps*, or flat pictures of the earth's surface.

The earth is about 8,000 miles across. This means the earth has millions of square miles of surface. In order to find exactly where something is on that surface, we need some guides.

A major guideline is known as the *equator.* This line runs east and west around the very center of the earth. The equator divides the

earth into two halves, or *hemispheres:* the northern hemisphere and the southern hemisphere.

At the very northern point on the earth is the *North Pole.* The *South Pole* is at the most southern point on earth. Locating something on or near the equator or either of the poles is quite easy. But what about finding places in between?

A degree is a way of measuring distance around a circle or sphere. Every circle or sphere contains 360 degrees. Since the earth is a sphere, it contains 360 degrees. The distance from the North Pole to the South Pole is halfway around the earth. Therefore there are 180 degrees between the North Pole and South Pole. Another way of looking at this is to see that there are 180 degrees from the equator over a pole and back to the equator.

To locate places between the equator and the poles, it helps to know how many degrees north or south of the equator those places are. The equator is the starting point for counting degrees north and south. Its location could be written as 0°. The poles are 90 degrees north or south of the equator. Their location is usually written as 90°.

> **Think About It:**
> What would be the location, in degrees, of a city exactly halfway between the equator and the North Pole?

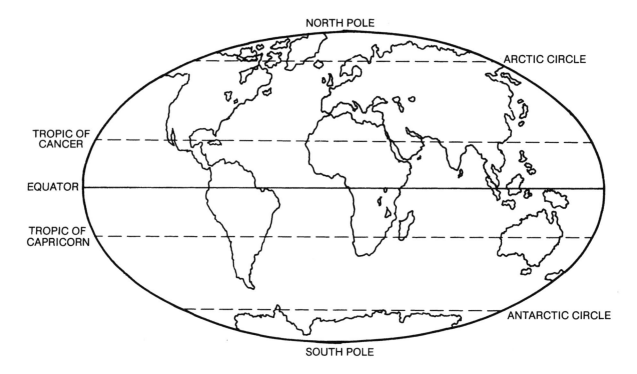

Lines are drawn on maps and globes that are parallel to the equator. The lines are called lines of *latitude*. They are also known as *parallels of latitude*. These lines are one degree apart north and south of the equator.

Locations for places north or south of the equator are given in degrees of latitude. Cairo, Egypt, for example, is 30° north latitude. This means that Cairo is 30 degrees north of the equator.

The *Tropic of Cancer* and the *Tropic of Capricorn* are special parallels of latitude that are $23\frac{1}{2}°$ north and south of the equator. Two other special parallels are $66\frac{1}{2}°$ north and south of the equator. They are the *Arctic Circle* and the *Antarctic Circle*.

Parallels or lines of latitude are fine for locating places north or south of the equator. But what about finding our way east and west around the earth?

The earth is divided into an eastern half and a western half, or hemisphere. The *Prime Meridian* runs from the North Pole to the South Pole through Greenwich, England. It is used as the starting point for measuring east and west around the globe.

All meridian lines run from the North Pole to the South Pole. They are usually called lines of *longitude*. These lines are located one degree apart from each other all the way around the globe.

There are 180 lines or degrees of longitude to the east of the Prime Meridian. Naturally, there are another 180 lines or degrees of longitude west of the Prime Meridian.

We can locate cities and nations by the number of degrees they are east or west of the Prime Meridian. Denver, Colorado, for example, is 105° west of the Prime Meridian.

The lines of latitude and longitude form what we call a *grid*. Once we know the number of degrees a place is north or south of the equator and east or west of the Prime Meridian, we can locate it on a map or globe.

More Information About Maps

To understand the information shown on a map, we need to know several things. One of the very important things we have to know is *direction*. It doesn't do much good to look at a map and have no idea whether one city is north or south of another. For this reason, maps sometimes have an arrow or *compass* telling the map user which direction is north. Unless a map's arrow tells you otherwise, north is always located at the top of a map.

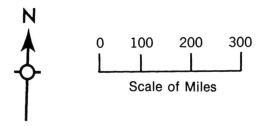

In order to know just how large a section of the earth a map shows, we need a *scale of distance*. A scale of distance is a line that looks quite a bit like a little ruler. Each section on the scale of distance stands for a certain number of miles or kilometers on the earth's surface.

The earth is about 25,000 miles around at the equator. Maps may be a few feet across or even only inches across. Therefore, an inch on a map may stand for hundreds or even thousands of miles on earth.

A small map that shows one entire hemisphere might have a scale of distance in which one inch stands for several thousand miles. A map the same size that shows a small nation might use a scale in which one inch represents ten or twenty miles.

At times, the scale of distance is written out in words rather than shown as a line divided into sections. Such a written scale might say, "One inch equals one hundred miles."

Maps often show *time zones.* By dividing the 360 degrees in a circle by the 24 hours in a day, we learn that an hour is 15 degrees. In other words, every 15 degrees from east to west on the earth, the time changes by 1 hour.

Sometimes, the time zones are marked by little clock faces at the top of the map. These clocks point to different times in different zones. Their purpose is to help the map user compare the time in one place with the time in another.

Maps that show national *borders* are called *political* maps. These maps often include important cities as well. Political maps often use color or shading to help the map user tell one nation or region from another.

Some maps show *physical features.* Mountain ranges, rivers, deserts, and lakes are common physical features. Some of these features may also appear on political maps.

Special maps may tell how much rainfall, or *precipitation*, an area gets each year. Other special maps show average temperatures. *Population density* maps give the user an idea how close people live to each other.

Still other maps tell what crops are grown or what languages are spoken in nations or regions.

The more you use maps, the easier they are to understand. Maps are a big help in learning about the history of the world.

A Quick Review

Read each statement in this quick review of what you have learned about maps. Decide whether the statement is true or false. Write "true" or "false" in the space before each statement.

_____   1. Our earth is a sphere.

_____   2. The equator divides the earth into east and west hemispheres.

_____   3. Lines of latitude are parallel to the equator.

_____   4. The Arctic Circle is south of the equator.

_____   5. The Prime Meridian runs through Denver, Colorado.

_____   6. Maps are usually drawn with north at the top.

_____   7. A scale of distance is always shown in kilometers.

_____   8. Political maps often use color or shading to show borders.

_____   9. Mountains and rivers are physical features.

_____   10. The world has 26 time zones.

THE FIRST CIVILIZED PEOPLE

Introduction

Inventions and discoveries through the ages have allowed us more and more wonderful choices of how to live. Let's look back in time and see how some early people lived. Let's also see what things they did then that help us live the way we do now.

The People of Sumer

Nearly 7,000 years ago, the people of *Sumer* lived where the country of Iraq is today. These people, called Sumerians, built their cities in the valleys along the *Tigris* and the *Euphrates rivers.* They settled along the rivers because of the rich soil and water supply. About nine out of every ten people farmed. The others were businesspeople, priests, rulers, or traders. Slaves were used by farmers and merchants.

The Sumerians were the first people known to use *irrigation. Irrigation* is the term for getting water to fields when there isn't enough rain to grow crops. The Sumerians dug large ditches and ponds. When the river flooded, the ponds filled. When dry weather came, ditches carried water from the ponds to the fields. Without irrigation the people of Sumer could not have raised large crops.

The earliest surviving examples of *writing* are Sumerian. At first the Sumerians used picture writing, but it was too slow and hard to use. They then invented a kind of writing called *cuneiform.* A wedge-shaped stick was used to make marks in wet clay *tablets.* The

clay was then hardened by baking to make a lasting record. Writing made record keeping possible. It also enabled one city to send messages to another.

The Sumerians had a *government.* Every nation needs some form of government. At first each city had its own government. These cities were small *city-states.* The city-states soon learned to cooperate. They formed one nation, ruled by a king. The stronger nation could better protect itself during war. Because all cities helped with trade and irrigation, the nation could live better.

Any nation needs *laws* to live peacefully. Sumer had some interesting laws. Anyone who said a person had committed a crime had to prove it. If not, the accuser could be put to death. If your leg was cut in a fight, you had the right to cut your enemy's leg. The laws also divided the population into three classes: aristocrats, commoners, and slaves. Slaves had rights and could even own land. Sometimes a slave could buy his or her freedom. On the other hand, for some crimes a free person could be made a slave.

Religion was important to the Sumerians. They built huge temples of clay bricks and believed that their priests could talk to the gods. The Sumerian religion told about the gods creating human beings. Their religion told the story of a great flood. Some of the gods decided to destroy the people on earth by a great flood. A favored king of one city was warned by friendly gods, so he built a great boat. In this great boat the good king took all the animals of the field and forest.

After the rain stopped and the flood waters went down, the good king gave thanks to the friendly gods who had warned him. Flood stories like this one are found in many cultures.

The Sumerians studied *science* and *math*. The Sumerians may well have been the first to use the *wheel*. Another of their inventions was the sailboat. They studied *astronomy* and knew when the seasons of the year were coming. Days were divided into hours, and each hour had sixty minutes. Only wealthy boys went to school. They had classes in arithmetic, reading, history, and geography.

The Sumerians developed systems of measurement. Because they were farming communities, they needed a way to measure land accurately. So they created one. Because they used silver money, they developed a way to use weights and measures on a scale to find the value of their coins.

Think About It:
Sumer is the first known civilization. What do we know about Sumer that might make us wonder if it really was the first civilization?

The Sumerians knew how to build. They used curved *arches* to make doorways. *Columns* to hold up roofs came from Sumer, too. They built palaces and temples of baked-clay bricks.

The earliest known map also came from ancient Sumer. The map was scratched into a clay tablet. It showed the Euphrates, one of the two major rivers of Sumer.

Think About It:
What six or eight things about Sumer remind you of the United States today? What two or three things are different from our way of life now?

The Land of the Nile

Just as the people of Sumer settled along rivers, so did the people of Egypt. The *Nile River* helped *Egypt* get its start. When the Nile flooded each spring, it covered the farms with rich soil. When the dry season came, water was lifted out of the Nile into irrigation ditches. Then, as today, the Nile brought life to the farmers of Egypt.

Just as in Sumer, a number of towns joined together to make one nation. Egypt's ruler was called a *pharaoh*, which means "great house." He made laws, led the army, and was head of the religion. It was believed the pharaoh was a kind of god. There were many gods in addition to the pharaoh, however.

Think About It:
Why would the people of Egypt be likely to obey any orders given by the pharaoh?

As in Sumer, most of the people were poor. They were farmers or soldiers. The few people who made up the upper class were priests, landowners, and rulers. Slaves came at the bottom of the social ladder. Slaves were sometimes war captives and sometimes just people who had had trouble with the law.

Trade was important to Egypt. Egypt traded with cities along the Mediterranean Sea. However, Egyptians also used the Red Sea to set sail toward the East. Most of their trade was *barter.* This meant they traded one thing for another and didn't use money.

Pyramid and Sphinx, Egypt

The Egyptians studied science and math. They may have been the first to use addition, subtraction, and division. They knew how to get medicine from plants. They derived a calendar of 365 days to help them keep track of the yearly flooding of the Nile. Because of this yearly flood, they had to learn how to measure land when boundary markers got washed out. For this they used basic ideas of *geometry.*

Writing was different in Egypt. The people used *hieroglyphics*, or picture writing. Since this system was complicated, only a few people in Egypt learned to read and write. Only the sons of the rich went to school to become priests, rulers, or scribes (record keepers). Most people had little use for reading and writing.

We have the Egyptians to thank for early paper. It was made from a reed called *papyrus.* This same plant was used to make riverboats. In 1969 and again in 1970, the famous explorer Thor Heyerdahl used a boat made of papyrus bundles to sail the Atlantic Ocean.

Think About It:
Egypt and Sumer both had strong governments. The people of these nations invented and discovered many things. How did government help invention and discoveries to happen?

Like the Sumerians, the people of Egypt believed in a life after death. Egyptian *mummies* were dead bodies wrapped in cloth and treated with drugs to preserve them. The Egyptians wanted the dead person to be ready for a new life. For this reason, bodies of the rich and powerful were placed in *tombs.* The great *pyramids* are the largest of these tombs. Food, servants, clothing, and tools were often buried with the rich person's body.

The Egyptians left beautiful samples of art. Paintings in tombs can still be seen. Huge statues hundreds of feet high were carved of stone. Egyptian artists made small statues and figures of famous people or religious symbols.

Many Egyptians wore makeup, dyed their hair, and wore fingernail polish. Music and dances were enjoyed. Chariot races were popular, along with hunting and fishing. Of course, the rich enjoyed more of these things than the poor. The poor were too busy making a living to have time for much else. Women were expected to raise the children and look after the house. Many women also worked in the fields. However, by law, women had the same rights as men. If he treated her badly, a woman could even take her husband to court!

Think About It:
Do you see any things in ancient Egypt that might make you think of your life today? What are they?

Review Exercise

Fifteen statements related to your reading are listed below. A blank follows each statement. If the statement is true for only Sumer, write 1 in the blank. If the statement is true for only Egypt, write 2 in the blank. Put 3 in the blank if the statement is true for both Sumer and Egypt.

1. The cities were usually along a river.   _____

2. The farmers used irrigation during the dry season.   _____

3. The people believed the ruler was a god.   _____

4. Cuneiform writing was used.   _____

5. Huge tombs called pyramids were built for dead leaders.   _____

6. Laws were developed.   _____

7. The people believed in a life after death.   _____

8. Math and science were studied.   _____

9. Rich boys went to school.   _____

10. Temples and palaces were built of clay bricks.   _____

11. A kind of paper was made from reeds.   _____

12. People knew about the seasons of the year.   _____

13. Few people were in the rich upper class.   _____

14. The dead were preserved as mummies.   _____

15. The people owned slaves.   _____

Now look back over your answers. Do you have twice as many 2's as 1's? You should have! Add the 1's, 2's, and 3's all together. Do you get a total of 37? If you don't, either you have some wrong answers or you didn't add correctly.

Early African Civilizations

The people of Egypt shared Africa with other early civilizations. The others were not anything like Egypt, however. The huge *Sahara Desert* separated other African people from Egypt.

One civilization lived in West Africa. The *Nok* people lived in the northern part of what is now *Nigeria*. There were many Nok people because they lived in a *fertile* area that produced enough food to feed them. The Noks also learned to use *iron* to make better weapons and tools.

Most early African people did not belong to large empires like Egypt. Many lived in small villages and farmed. They raised *crops* including grains, yams, and bananas. The *herders* moved from place to place to find feed for their cattle and other livestock.

Farmers and herders were alike in several ways. They did not have *governments,* but they did have rules for their people. They didn't have rulers, but the wise people in their groups were leaders.

These early people formed the basis for the African *empires* discussed later.

Who Else Lived Near Egypt and Sumer?

As the years went by, Sumer was named *Assyria* and then *Babylon.* The name depended upon what group of people had *conquered* the Sumerians. Egypt was always Egypt, but it too was defeated in war by other nations.

North of Sumer is an area called *Asia Minor,* where Turkey is today. About 2,000 B.C., people called the *Hittites* lived in Asia Minor. These people learned to read and write from both Sumer and Egypt. Their religion and laws were similar to those of Sumer. But the Hittites had something neither Egypt nor Sumer had. They had *iron.* Weapons made of iron were much stronger than the *copper* weapons of Egypt. Using iron weapons and chariots pulled by fast horses, the Hittites were able to beat most nations in battle. But just like other warlike nations, the Hittites finally were defeated and their nation ended.

About the time the Hittites were winning battles, the *Hebrew* people moved into the land at the eastern end of the Mediterranean Sea. They conquered *Palestine,* a small nation that was about where Israel is today. These people were one of the first to worship just

one god. They wrote about their history and their religion in the *Old Testament* of the *Bible.* The Hebrew people divided their kingdom into two parts. Once divided, it became weak and was taken over by others.

Torah covers

The world's first great explorers lived just north of Palestine. The people of *Phoenicia* used their fine trees to build trading ships. These ships took them all along the shores of the Mediterranean and into the Atlantic Ocean. Phoenician sailors sailed along the coast of Africa to the south and as far as Britain to the north. Wherever they went, they set up colonies and traded with the people they met. They traded their fine handblown glass and beautiful handmade cloth with other nations. The purple dye they made was used only for royal clothing because it was so expensive.

One important thing the Phoenicians did was to complete an *alphabet* based on Egyptian principles. They came up with the idea of making words by putting letters together in different ways. The alphabet used to write this page is based on the one the Phoenicians created some 3,000 years ago!

Think About It:
All successful nations knew how to write.
Why was writing so important to a nation?

Some nations are never happy with the land they have. *Persia* was such a nation. Starting about 550 B.C., the Persians made war on the entire world they knew. During the next 200 years, nations such as Egypt were beaten by Persia's huge army. Persia's great leader, *Cyrus the Great*, led his armies as far east as India. The Persians had a clever strategy to help them govern the lands they took in battle. Fine *roads* were built to join all parts of their kingdom. Messengers carrying important news could change horses every few miles along these roads. It was like the American Pony Express, only a couple of thousand years earlier!

Think About It:
Good weapons help nations conquer others. Using an alphabet speeds up communication. Good roads help unite a nation. Which of these is most important to a civilization and why?

Like so many other nations, Persia borrowed good ideas from other peoples. Persians collected *taxes*, just as did the rulers of Egypt. They believed in life after death, as did the Egyptians and Sumerians. Many of their laws were like those of Sumer.

Think About It:
Was religion important to the early people from Sumer and Persia? How do you know it was or was not?
Why do nations collect taxes? Early nations did, and so do nations today. Why do you think this might be?

Hammurabi

When his father died, Hammurabi took the throne of Babylon. At that time, around 2,000 B.C., Mesopotamia was divided among several small city-states. Mesopotamia is the area between the Tigris and Euphrates rivers.

In the sixth year of his reign, Hammurabi fought a series of wars to win more land and keep other city-states from challenging Babylon.

Fine buildings were constructed, and living conditions improved for people in the city. Hammurabi made agreements with city-states around Babylon to solve problems peacefully.

Babylon did not stay at peace. A ruler of southern Mesopotamia went to war with Hammurabi. Hammurabi was helped by two northern kingdoms and won the war.

Two years later, Babylon fought one of the northern kingdoms and won that war. Soon afterwards, Babylon attacked and defeated its other former friend. Now Hammurabi controlled the land from the Persian Gulf on the south to the Assyrian Empire on the north.

Hammurabi ruled his large empire personally. He wanted to be sure his people were ruled fairly and well. One of Hammurabi's major duties was to be sure the irrigation system in southern Mesopotamia was kept in working order. Without irrigation there would be no harvests.

In order to help his people know what was expected of them, Hammurabi set up a list of laws. He also decided on punishments when laws were broken. This list of laws and punishments was the Code of Hammurabi. Hammurabi had the laws written so all could know them. Hammurabi's Code contained 282 laws. These laws applied to all people, whether rich or poor.

Most of these laws told what happened if a law was broken. "If a man stole the property of a god or of the king, that man shall be killed."

Hammurabi gave women rights as well. If a man divorced his wife, he had to take care of the children and give back her dowry. Married women could own and manage property.

Hammurabi lived almost 4,000 years ago. However, he did a lot that made the legal system usable even for people living today.

China and India Begin

As early as 4500 B.C., Chinese civilization was beginning. People began to settle into farming villages along the Huang He River, then along the Yangtze River as well. They tamed animals, using them to provide food and help with farming. Here, too, the rivers flooded. People learned how to irrigate during the dry season. They also used copper and bronze tools. Silk was already being made, and a writing system was developed.

Religion was an important part of Chinese life. The people believed their rulers were appointed by the gods. The rule was passed down from father to son in the same family. These ruling families were called *dynasties.* Many dynasties lasted for hundreds of years.

About 2,500 years ago, *Confucius* was born in China. He was a teacher and thinker. He developed a system of ethics, teaching people how to get along. His teachings had a deep effect on Chinese life. His system became known as *Confucianism.*

Great Confucian altar, Peking

Partway between China and Egypt is the *Indus River.* Along this river in what is now Pakistan, another group of people were living. They also farmed and used copper metal. They made cotton cloth, raised cattle, and used camels and buffalo. And of course, they could read and write. The only problem is, no one today can read their writing. Maybe someday you'll hear of someone who has finally figured out how to read their language.

> **Think About It:**
> Religion was important in early civilizations. So was some form of writing. How did they both help hold a civilization together?

It was in India that the *Hindu* religion began. Hindus believe in *reincarnation,* or rebirth. A person who lives a good life may return as a human, while a person who lives a bad life may return as an animal. For this reason, Hindus don't eat meat. They might be eating a person who has returned as an animal!

Another part of the Hindu religion was the *caste system.* You remember that Sumer and Egypt had classes of people. In those places people could move from one class to another if they worked hard enough. Hindu classes, or castes, were unchanging. If someone was born a high-caste person, he or she stayed that way. Low-caste people could not change their caste until they died and were reborn. If they had been good in this life, they were rewarded after death—they were reborn into a higher caste. This system was unfair, but it was a part of the Hindu religion. Today the caste system is outlawed, but many people in India still believe in it.

While Confucius lived in China, Buddha was born in India. The religion based on his beliefs spread to include most of eastern Asia. *Buddhism* teaches that desire causes pain. To get rid of pain, overcome desire and attachment to things of this earth. To do this, meditate and follow the Eightfold Path. This path names eight areas of life where it is important to do things right: knowledge, intention, speech, conduct, employment, effort, mindfulness, and concentration. The final goal is to achieve Nirvana, or the spirit's union with eternal harmony. Millions of people—especially in southern Asia, China, and Japan—still follow Buddha's teachings.

A Buddhist statue

Review Exercises

To answer the General Map and Cradles of Civilization Questions, you may find it helpful to use the map on page 16. If several answers are given, underline the correct one.

General Map Questions

1. Four oceans are shown on the map on page 16. Can you find them all? Write their names on the four lines below.

    a) _____   c) _____

    b) _____   d) _____

2. This ocean is located in the southern part of your map:
    a) Atlantic b) Indian c) Pacific d) Arctic

3. The ocean on the east side of this map is:
    a) Atlantic b) Indian c) Pacific d) Arctic

4. The _____ ocean is located so far north of the equator that it is almost always ice-covered.

5. There are three continents on this map.

    a. The continent entirely surrounded by the thick line is _____ .

    b. Northwest of the continent you named in a) above and connected to it by land is another continent:
        1) Europe 2) Asia 3) Africa

    c. The continents of Europe and Africa are separated by this body of water:
        1) Atlantic Ocean 2) Mediterranean Sea 3) Red Sea 4) Persian Gulf

    d. _____ is the biggest continent shown on the map.
        1) Asia 2) Europe 3) Africa

    e. The smallest continent shown on the map is _____ .

Cradles of Civilization Questions

1. The first known civilization started along the Tigris and the Euphrates rivers. The name of this civilization was:

   _____.

2. Probably the best-known early civilization was Egypt. This civilization started along

   the _____ River.

3. Three of the earliest civilizations developed on the same continent. What is the name of this continent?
   a) Europe b) Asia c) Africa

4. The only continent shown on the map that didn't have one of the four earliest

   civilizations is _____.

5. Three of these civilizations may have traded together, using rivers or other bodies of water for traveling. Which one is too far away to have known about, or traded with, the other three?
   a) Egypt b) Sumer c) Indus d) Huang He or China

6. One part of the Nile River starts in Lake Victoria and flows into the Mediterranean Sea. In which direction would you be traveling if you traveled with the river to the Mediterranean Sea? (Remember: the top of the map is north.)
   a) east b) west c) north d) south

7. The _____ river flows into the Pacific Ocean.

8. If you traveled along the _____ river, you would travel southwest.

9. Which of the four early civilizations is the farthest from the equator?
   a) Egypt b) Sumer c) Indus d) Huang He or China

10. Look at the scale of miles on the map. If you could travel from Egypt to Sumer in a straight line, about how many miles would it be?
    a) 200 b) 400 c) 600 d) 800

11. Using the same scale of miles, figure out about how long the Nile River is from Lake Victoria to the Mediterranean Sea.
    a) 800 b) 1,200 c) 1,600 d) 2,000

12. The scale of miles shows the Tigris River to be about how long?
    a) 400 b) 600 c) 800 d) 1,000

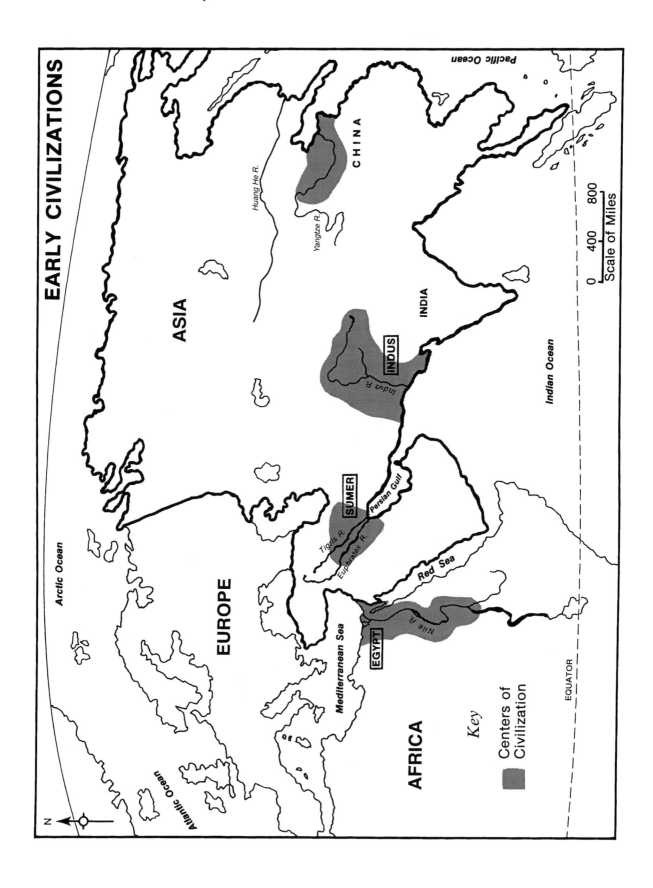

Puzzle Quiz

Each of the following clues should make you think of a word from this unit. When necessary, look back over the unit to see which word in bold italics matches the clue. Be sure each answer you choose fits the puzzle spaces exactly.

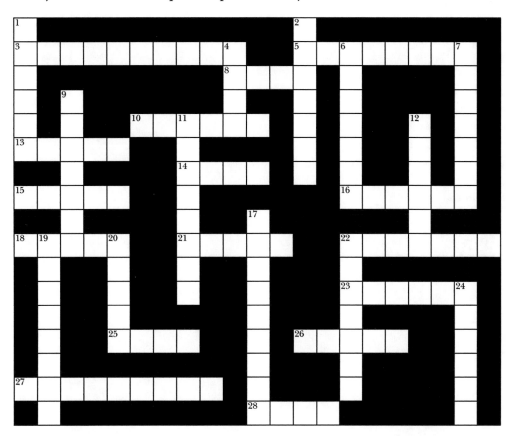

Across

3. Use of ditches to water crops during dry seasons
5. A system of letters invented by the Phoenicians to make writing easier
8. Metal used by the Hittites to make weapons
10. Trading one item for another when money isn't used
13. The first civilization where Iraq is today
14. Rules for living with one another
15. What hieroglyhpics were used to do
16. A people who don't eat meat for religious reasons
18. An Indian system of classes
21. The river where ancient Indian civilization began
22. Huge tomb for Egyptian pharaoh
23. Nation that built roads over its lands for armies and messengers
25. Burial place for wealthy Egyptian
26. _____ the Great led Persian armies as far as India
27. Great Chinese teacher
28. Study of numbers, short form

Down

1. River near the Euphrates, where Sumer began
2. River along which early Chinese people lived
4. River depended on by the Egyptian people
6. Egyptian ruler
7. Pieces of clay upon which the Sumerians wrote
9. Preserved bodies of dead Egyptians
11. Worship of a god or gods
12. Religious leader born in India
17. Kind of writing done in Sumer
19. A relative who lived before you
20. Nation whose people believed their ruler was a god
22. Writing material like paper
24. Curved tops of windows or doors that made buildings stronger

GREECE
AND
ROME

Introduction

Two nations on the Mediterranean Sea achieved greatness. Greece came first; Rome followed. Much of Western civilization today has been strongly influenced by the things these people learned and did many years ago.

The people of these two civilizations had many great ideas. They also made some mistakes. When you are reading about these people, watch for both. Learning about mistakes that the Greeks and Romans made 2,000 years ago might keep us from repeating them.

The Early Greeks

When trading ships sailed from Egypt and Phoenicia, they often stopped at the island of *Crete*. This large island in the Mediterranean Sea was where one of the greatest nations in the ancient world began. Ships from Crete carried goods to other settlements along the Mediterranean. The sailors from Crete observed the customs and ways of other nations. They remembered useful ideas and took them home.

It wasn't long before the people of Crete developed their own kind of writing. They learned to make *pottery* and used new ideas to improve it. They learned to work with gold and ivory. Their jewelry was popular every-where.

Just as the Phoenicians had done, the people of Crete started colonies around the Mediterranean. Some of their colonies were in Greece, which later became the center of one of the greatest civilizations in the world. The people of Crete did well trading and prospered.

Most good things seem to end, however. For Crete, the end came when the stronger navy from Greece defeated the navy of Crete. By about 1000 B.C., the *Dorians* from Greece were using iron weapons and were very strong.

> **Think About It:**
> Why did Crete have a large navy but almost no army?

Just like Sumer, Crete and Greece began with city governments. The mountains of Greece divided the country into small areas. Each city had its own government and army. Some Greek rulers were kind, and some were harsh. Many Greek rulers forced the farmers to pay high taxes. Those who couldn't pay sometimes lost their land and were sold as slaves.

Some Greek states, such as *Sparta*, became very warlike. Men and boys in Sparta were trained to be soldiers able to withstand great hardships. Boys began military training when they were seven and stayed in the army until they were about thirty. The word "Spartan" today means "disciplined" or simple to the point of being uncomfortable.

Athens, another Greek state, started a kind of government called a *democracy*. Every voter helped rule the city. Free men over eighteen years old could vote. Women, children, and slaves couldn't vote in Athens. Even so, the government of Athens was something like today's democratic government in the United States.

Greece's Golden Age

About 500 B.C., Greece went to war against Persia. Athens eventually defeated Persia and began to change in a number of ways. The result is known as the *Golden Age* of Greece.

Nearly 200 city-states turned to Athens for leadership. Just as Sumer had brought city-states together, so did Greece. Athens protected smaller city-states and for a time was the center of one of the most advanced civilizations the world had ever known.

Laws were written out, and everyone knew what they were. People who owed money could not be sold as slaves. The rich no longer took land forcibly from the poor. A powerful navy protected Greece from other nations. Greek merchants sailed, looking for trade.

Under the leadership of Athens, life in Greece got better and better. Greek schools improved and taught such things as reading, math, music, and sports to boys. Girls didn't attend public school.

Great thinkers, called *philosophers*, begin to teach. *Philosopher* means "lover of wisdom." *Socrates* was a philosopher who thought one could discover the truth by asking the right questions. Others set up plans for government or studied science and medicine.

Many of the most beautiful marble buildings in the world were built by the Greeks of Athens. Statues we still wonder at today were carved during this time. Plays written and performed for the citizens of Athens are still read and enjoyed today. Other Greek authors

wrote poetry, social commentary, and books on education.

Greek Olympic Stadium

The *Olympic Games* started during this time. Every four years, *athletes* from all over Greece took part in running, jumping, wrestling, and other sports. If sports were ever more popular than they are today, it must have been in ancient Greece.

The people relied on the gods for help. The Greeks thought of their gods very much as people. Greek gods were supposed to have fought each other and to have had fun, just like the humans they controlled.

Life during Greece's Golden Age was wonderful if you were a rich citizen of Athens. However, slaves weren't as well off. Many suffered from overwork. Only a few were able to buy their freedom and become citizens. Women had few rights. The poor worked hard and had few pleasures. But all things considered, Greece's Golden Age provided its citizens with a good life.

Once again, war changed things. While the people of Athens had learned to enjoy a cultured life and good government, Sparta had stayed warlike. Finally war broke out between the two city-states of Greece. It took

Sparta 27 years to defeat Athens. Both states were left so weak they could no longer defend themselves against outsiders. The Golden Age of Greece was over!

> **Think About It:**
> Some civilizations had great cultures. Many of these were defeated in battle. Can nations today learn lessons from the defeats of past civilizations?

Soon after Athens and Sparta fought, a neighbor to the north began taking over the Greek city-states. *Philip*, King of Macedonia, finally controlled all of Greece. His son, *Alexander*, took over the army when Philip died. By the time Alexander died at 32, he had conquered most of the world he knew about. From Greece to Egypt to India, Alexander the Great ruled.

Alexander had many good ideas. He thought people from different nations should marry each other as a way of keeping peace among nations. People from all religions were welcome in his army and his nations. He set up a system of money so all parts of his kingdom could trade easily. He wanted people to be well educated. His own teacher had been *Aristotle*, a philosopher from Athens. Aristotle's teacher was Plato, and Plato was a student of Socrates, the great thinker we learned about earlier. During and after Alexander's time, Greek men learned much of astronomy and mathematics.

Despite Alexander's plans, his kingdom didn't last. When he died, his kingdom was divided. Not only had Greece's Golden Age ended, but also the time had come when Greece itself would no longer be free.

> **Think About It:**
> Name several things that Athens and the United States have in common. List a few differences.

Puzzle Quiz

Each description that follows has a one-word answer. The spaces following each clue stand for the letters in the answer. One letter in each answer is already in place.

1. Island nation in the Mediterranean Sea: __ __ e __ __ __

2. Warlike city-state in Greece: __ __ __ __ t __

3. Famous Greek thinker, or philosopher: __ __ __ __ a __ __ __

4. Powerful nation north of Greece: __ __ __ __ o __ __

5. Greek state where democracy began: __ __ __ e __ __

6. Macedonian king who conquered all Greece: __ __ __ __ i __

7. King of Macedonia who ruled the world of his time: __ __ __ a __ __ __ __

8. Athletic games held every four years in Greece: __ __ __ __ __ i __

9. The time when Greece was at its best is often called the ___ ___ of Greece: __ o __ __ __ __ __ __ __

10. Nation that was defeated by Macedonia: __ __ e __ __ __

Ancient Greece

Answer these questions with the help of the map on page 23. Put your answer in the blank to the left of the question.

When you've answered all the questions, try to locate the places again in the maze on page 24. Put a circle around each name in the maze. The words can go up or down. They may go across, and sometimes they are written backwards. Be careful! They can be tricky!

_____ 1. Five different seas are shown on the map. Look carefully at each one to find the smallest.

_____ 2. This sea is found in the northwestern corner of the map.

_____ 3. This narrow channel, or strait, separates the Black Sea from the Sea of Marmara.

_____ 4. If you travel from the Aegean Sea to the Sea of Marmara, you go through a narrow channel, or strait. This strait is called the Dardanelles today. What did the Greeks call it?

_____ 5. Most of Asia Minor was not controlled by Greece. Who did control Asia Minor?

_____ 6. The Olympic Games are held every four years. They were first started in Greece. Find the city whose name will tell you that the Olympic Games started there.

_____ 7. The city of Sparta is found on this peninsula.

_____ 8. South of Greece is a large island. What is the island's name?

_____ 9. West of Greece is part of another peninsula. Name this peninsula.

_____ 10. If the people of Athens traveled to the city of Troy, they would have gone over this sea.

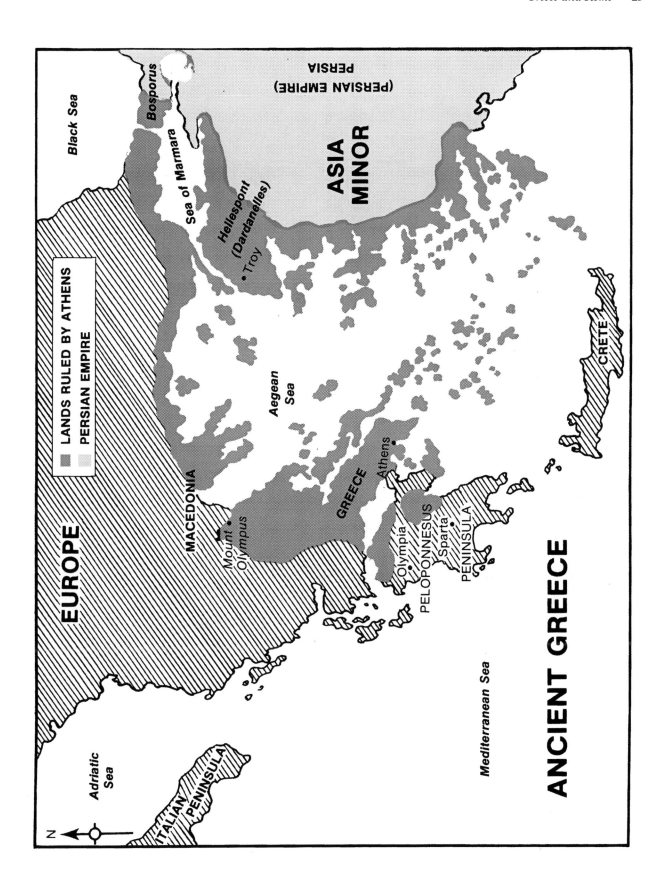

ANCIENT GREECE

LANDS RULED BY ATHENS

PERSIAN EMPIRE

Now, here's the letter maze. Can you find all the answers in it?

E	S	A	S	E	T	E	Q	U	I	A	O
S	E	N	W	R	H	E	S	T	O	N	P
W	A	D	R	I	A	T	I	C	S	E	A
R	O	T	D	I	E	C	B	K	T	R	D
T	F	N	R	T	G	A	C	W	A	S	S
F	M	O	I	A	E	O	A	L	P	U	E
W	A	P	I	T	A	L	I	A	N	R	U
B	R	S	E	C	N	Y	T	E	O	O	R
C	M	E	S	I	S	M	A	T	A	P	O
N	A	L	T	A	E	P	E	E	I	S	A
E	R	L	L	I	A	I	A	R	S	O	S
I	A	E	A	N	C	A	I	C	R	B	U
A	T	H	U	S	T	T	E	E	B	P	R
T	P	E	R	S	I	A	N	P	O	S	O
P	E	L	O	P	O	N	N	E	S	U	S

Alexander the Great

Follow Alexander the Great in his conquests. Fill in the answers to the questions about Alexander by looking either on the map on page 25 or in the reading.

1. Alexander was born in the country of Macedonia. (Find Macedonia on the map.) South of Macedonia is the country of _____. Two important Greek cities shown on the map are _____ and _____.

2. After capturing Greece, Alexander moved into Asia Minor. What body of water is north of Asia Minor? _____ What country controlled Asia Minor until Alexander took it away? _____

3. The country of Persia lies between a sea and a gulf. What are the names of these two bodies of water? _____ and _____ .

4. While Alexander was conquering Persia, he also captured two of the areas where civilization first started. These two river valleys around Persia were the _____ on the east and the _____ on the west. Both of these, as well as Persia, are on the continent of _____ .

5. After defeating Persia, Alexander conquered a third ancient civilization. This one grew up west of the Red Sea, along the _____ River. This civilization was called _____ .

6. If Macedonia is on the continent of Europe, Alexander controlled land on how many continents? _____ These continents are named _____, _____ , and _____ .

7. The mountains that seem to stretch from the Black Sea to the Caspian Sea are called the _____ .

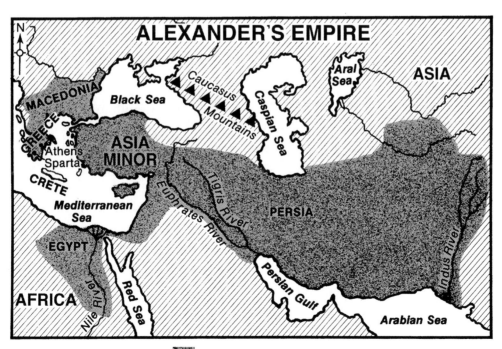

Alexander's Empire

Pericles

Pericles was born in Athens, Greece, about 495 B.C. His father was a famous warrior. His mother was the niece of a famous statesman named Cleisthenes.

Cleisthenes brought many democratic reforms to Athens. He had given the assembly and courts the power to govern. Pericles wanted to continue these reforms. He joined the popular party and began his work.

In 463 B.C., Pericles was a state prosecutor who helped try Cimon, a powerful general. Cimon wanted Athens to join with its enemy, Sparta. Pericles lost the trial but became famous among the people of Athens.

Pericles helped the people gain power by giving power to the Council of Five Hundred, the popular court, and the assembly. When the party leader was killed, Pericles took his place.

Pericles was elected one of the ten generals of Athens. Each year for nearly 30 years, he was reelected.

Pericles brought about changes in the government of Athens. He decided government officers should be paid. This meant poor people could afford to hold office.

Pericles' goal was to make Athens a powerful democracy. Athens had a strong navy, but Pericles wanted it to have a strong army as well. Pericles started a series of wars to gain more land. He did not always win. As a result, Cimon took charge of the

armies. Cimon defeated Persia in 449 B.C. and died soon afterwards.

Three years later Athens signed a 30-year peace treaty with Sparta. This gave Athens control of a league of Greek cities that joined together for trade. Pericles used money from the league to build up the navy and make Athens beautiful. The Parthenon was built at this time.

War with Sparta came in 431 B.C. Much of the land around Athens was lost. Then a year later, plague broke out and killed many people. Pericles was blamed for the troubles of Athens and removed from power.

He was reelected the next year but did not rule long. Pericles died of the plague soon after his reelection.

The Rise of Rome

Alexander the Great had planned to march west to *Italy* after he finished with Persia. He died before this plan was carried out. As it turned out, armies from Italy marched east and took over much of the land Alexander had owned.

Italy had been settled by people from the north, from Asia Minor, and from Greece. The northerners were called *Latins*. They learned much from other peoples. They worshiped the Greek gods, though they gave these gods new names. Writing and government were also modeled after the Greeks. The people of Asia Minor taught them to build good roads. All these things helped the people of Italy.

Like so many other places, the Italian peninsula was dotted with many city-states. The city of *Rome* was more powerful than any other. Because it was built on seven hills, it was protected from its enemies. It used this safety to become a center of trade for most of Italy. By 270 B.C., Rome had taken control of most of the other city-states. It made these cities pay taxes to Rome and supply soldiers for Rome's army. In return, Rome protected them from attack by other nations.

Rome began to look for more lands to control. War broke out between Rome and *Carthage* in northern Africa. Carthage had been a Phoenician colony and had become strong. This war lasted off and on for 62 years. Finally Rome destroyed Carthage and was on its way to becoming more powerful. During the 75 years that followed, Rome fought and defeated Macedonia, Spain, and Greece. Roman rule went as far as Asia Minor and Egypt. The Hebrew nation of Palestine also became part of the Roman Empire.

When Rome captured an area, it was made a *province*. This meant that Rome governed it and received tax money and soldiers from that area. Many Romans in government used this tax money for their own good and became very wealthy. These wealthy people then bought large farms and used slaves to do the work. In this way they became even wealthier. As more and more slaves were used for work, the poor people couldn't find jobs. This soon led to troubles for Rome.

Rome Becomes Great

One of Rome's many accomplishments was a new kind of government. The people of Rome formed a *republic*, which is a government elected by the people. As in Greece, the wealthy people had the most to say about government. They elected the men who formed the *Senate*. These lawmakers were elected for life. The senators also chose two *consuls* to rule Rome for a year at a time.

At first, the poor people had little to say about the government of Rome. Finally, a plan was worked out to include the common people. They could choose two tribunes to represent them. If the tribunes felt a law was bad for the common people, they could turn it down, no matter what the Senate said. The tribunes also had the laws written down so everyone knew just what they were.

Most tribunes tried hard to help the people. Sometimes, though, when a tribune tried too hard, members of the Senate would have him murdered. One famous tribune killed himself when he heard the plans for his murder.

Roman schools were an improvement over those of other nations. They helped both to carry on the knowledge of the Greeks and to encourage new ideas. These schools trained boys to become lawyers, bookkeepers, and government workers. Boys stayed in school until they were 16. Even girls went to school until the age of 13. Education helped Rome become great.

Romans developed a new language. *Latin* was spoken by Romans and all the people they conquered. Many modern languages, such as French, Spanish, Italian, and Portuguese, came from Latin. For many hundreds of years, Latin was the language used by writers all over Europe. It is still the official language of the Catholic Church all over the world. Many prescriptions written by doctors today are still written in Latin. And many lawyers use Latin for legal terms.

Rome became great for other reasons as well. Roman law spread over all the world the Romans knew. The Roman calendar was better than older calendars and remained in use for over a thousand years. Rome followed the example of Persia and made roads connecting all parts of the empire. Some of these roads are still used even though they are 2,000 years old! Many Roman buildings still stand, too. Roman *aqueducts* for carrying water from the mountains to the cities are still bringing water to thirsty people in Rome today.

Think About It:
The Romans used ideas from other cultures. They also came up with fresh ideas. How did they blend the past and present to make their nation strong?

The Roman Forum

Roman Empire Puzzle Quiz

Use the map on page 33 to answer the questions below. Put the correct answers in the puzzle.

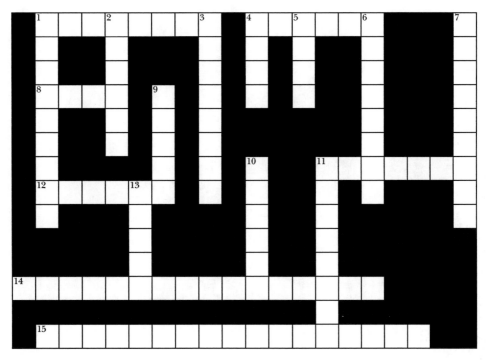

Across

1. This ocean is found west of the country of Gaul.
4. This continent is found south of the Mediterranean Sea.
8. This river in Africa starts in the south and flows north to empty into the Mediterranean Sea.
11. The Roman Empire controlled only half of this large island off the northern coast of Europe.
12. Which of these controlled the most land: the Roman *Republic* or the *Empire*?
14. This body of water was surrounded by the Roman Empire (2 words).
15. This narrow channel separates Spain from Africa (3 words).

Down

1. This chain of mountains runs along the Italian peninsula.
2. This famous Greek city-state is shown on the map.
3. South of the island of Sardinia was this city-state, which was destroyed by Rome.
4. These mountains lie between Italy and Gaul.
5. This city was the center of the Roman Empire.
6. This sea lies between Italy and Greece.
7. This peninsula lies south of the Black Sea (2 words).
9. This large island is found south of Greece.
10. Most of the Roman Empire lies on this continent.
11. The Danube River flows into this body of water (2 words).
13. This is one of the rivers near the northern border of the Roman Empire.

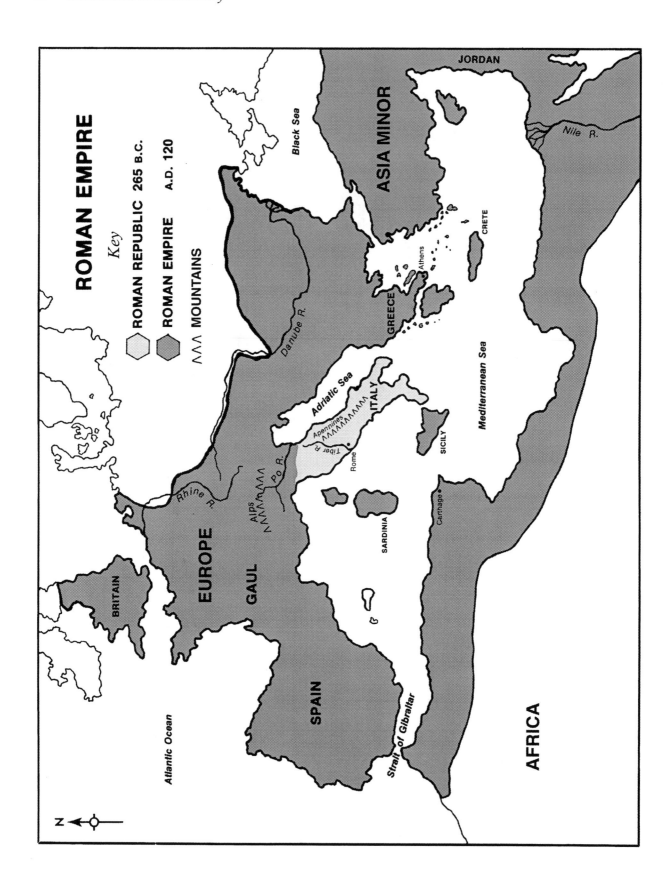

ROMAN EMPIRE

Key

ROMAN REPUBLIC 265 B.C.

ROMAN EMPIRE A.D. 120

ΛΛ MOUNTAINS

Rome's Decline

Rome started to have troubles while it was still growing. Romans began to use more and more slaves to do their work. Because of this, many unemployed people became angry about the lack of jobs. The government of Rome set up a large *welfare* system. It provided food for the hungry. To keep these people from thinking about their problems, the government set up free public entertainment. This entertainment was most likely to be a chariot race or an afternoon of fights in the *arena.*

Professional fighters were known as *gladiators.* Often these gladiators were strong slaves trained to fight. A gladiator had a good reason for wanting to win. If he lost, he might well be killed! Gladiators fought each other or wild animals. When *Christians* first appeared in Rome, they were often forced to fight the gladiators or the lions.

During this time, Rome was growing. Under the great general *Julius Caesar,* its armies had won *Gaul* and marched and sailed as far as *Britain.* These two areas are now called France and the United Kingdom, but for many years they were just provinces in the *Roman Empire.*

Julius Caesar took over Rome's government. Like many men before and after him, Julius Caesar found that good generals aren't always popular *politicians.* He passed many laws to help the poor. When the wealthy Romans thought he had done too much for the poor, they had him killed.

Augustus followed Julius Caesar as Rome's ruler. He was careful not to anger the Senate too much. Instead, he worked out a better plan of government for the Roman Empire. He tried hard to make government honest and helpful to the people. This must have been a good idea because Rome was at peace for about 200 years after this.

During this time a new religion had its beginnings in the Hebrew nation of Palestine. This religion, based on the teachings of Jesus Christ, was called *Christianity.* The Romans ruled Palestine. A Roman court ordered Christ put to death, and Roman soldiers carried out the court's order.

After the death of Christ, his followers, or *apostles,* spread his teachings. Many Romans felt Christianity offered them more than did their old gods. Christianity spread throughout much of the Roman Empire. In spite of the fact that Roman leaders killed many early Christians, the nation of Rome finally accepted Christianity as its official religion.

Even though things looked pretty good, Rome was weakening. The Romans had too many slaves and had grown lazy. Far too many people were on welfare or were supported by the government. The Romans spent too much money on armies and raised taxes too high in order to pay for the cost of the armies and the government. In order to raise more money, the government started mixing copper with the silver in its coins.

Think About It:
Rome was extremely powerful. Yet it declined and was destroyed. What lessons could modern nations learn from Rome?

The Roman Empire was divided into two parts. The eastern part lasted a thousand years longer than the western part. By A.D. 476, the western part had been destroyed. Fierce tribes of warlike people from the north attacked Rome. The *Visigoths* and the *Vandals* finally destroyed the city of Rome itself. These tribes had not been part of Rome. They ended the great Roman Empire because Rome had gotten weak and lazy.

Think About It:
The Roman leaders gave the poor "bread and circuses" to keep them happy. What does this mean?

Review Exercise

The nine questions below all have their answers hidden in the letter maze. Some of the answers are written across. Some go up and down. One is even backward. Some cross each other. Can you find all nine answers?

L	J	U	L	I	U	S	C	A	E	S	A	R
A	P	A	O	E	S	T	R	I	B	U	N	E
T	O	D	S	C	E	D	S	L	A	V	E	S
I	P	G	V	A	N	D	A	L	S	U	S	N
N	E	B	G	L	A	D	I	A	T	O	R	S
C	H	R	I	S	T	I	A	N	I	T	Y	T
F	A	R	A	I	E	G	A	H	T	R	A	C

1. What new language was spoken in Rome? _____

2. What great Roman general captured Gaul and Britain?

   _____

3. What African nation did Rome fight? _____

4. What new religion came to Rome after the death of Christ?

   _____

5. "Vandalism" means destroying things. The name of what German tribe is the origin for this word?

   _____

6. What was the name of the lawmaking group that was elected for life?

   _____

7. What name was given to a man chosen to represent the common people in Rome's government?

   _____

8. What name means "professional fighter"? _____

9. What group of people did much of the work in Rome?

   _____

THE MIDDLE AGES

Introduction

After the fall of the Western Roman Empire, conditions in Europe began to get worse. For this reason, the period is often called the *Dark Ages*. Gradually, a new way of life called *feudalism* developed. Religion became so important that great Western armies marched toward Jerusalem to fight in the *Crusades*.

It was also during this time that the religion of *Islam* came into being. Marked changes in China and Japan occurred, and in North and South America, three great civilizations were becoming important.

What Happened to Eastern Rome?

When the western part of the Roman Empire fell to the invading German tribes, the eastern part of the Roman Empire remained strong. The eastern capital city of *Constantinople* was a thriving trading city. The government was well organized, and the leadership was firm. The Eastern Roman Empire, too, accepted the Christian religion.

After the split, the Eastern Roman Empire changed. Its name changed, too. The world began to know it as the *Byzantine Empire*. Traders from the Byzantine Empire went all over the world. Not only did they bring back cloth and spices, they also brought back new ideas. These ideas became part of the Byzantine way of life. The language changed also. Greek took the place of Latin. The Church

became the *Orthodox Church*. This religion eventually spread as far as Russia.

While the Byzantine Empire was taking back lands lost when Rome fell, something was happening in the Arab lands. *Muhammad* (who died in A.D. 632) had started a new religion, *Islam*. Followers of this religion are called *Muslims*. The rules for Islam are found in the *Koran*, the Muslim holy book. Muslims believe in one god, *Allah*. They pray to him five times a day. Muslims are to treat other Muslims as brothers. They are not to drink or gamble. The Muslims also believe it is their duty to show everyone the true way to worship God. Muslims are to bring people of other religions to Islam. If people won't join on their own, the Muslims feel they can use war to spread their religion.

Muslim armies took away much of the Byzantine Empire. Muslims also conquered much of northern Africa. Then they left Africa and invaded Spain. The Muslims living in Spain were called *Moors*. The Muslims also took land as far to the east as India.

In spite of their warlike ideas, the Muslims did much good. Their *Arabic* language is still used today. They built roads and even had a postal service. They read, studied, and copied the writings of the Greeks. It was because of this copying that many Greek ideas weren't lost when the Roman Empire fell. The Arabic number system they used is what we use today. Such stories as the *Arabian Nights* are popular to this day.

Muslim traders also traveled all over the world they knew. They carried ideas as well as goods with them. In fact, the people of Arabia were much better educated at that time than the people of Europe. Their advances in mathematics, medicine, astronomy, chemistry, and navigation would not be matched in Europe for centuries.

Think About It:
How is Islam like Christianity?

What of India, China, and the Eastern World?

When the Muslims reached India in 674, they found Buddhists and Hindus already there. During the years that followed, India was weak or strong depending upon the ruler. After a time, India split into many little states. Some states followed Buddhism. Others became Muslim or Hindu. War after war between states of different religions followed. India became even weaker. Later, when powerful outside nations decided to take over India, the country couldn't defend itself.

China had many of the same problems. For example, the first Chinese emperor burned all the books containing the teachings of Confucius. Shi Huangdi thought this

would keep the ideas of Confucius from weakening the Chinese people.

Up to this time, China had been broken into small areas. About 220 B.C., Shi Huangdi brought China together. He set up uniform money, laws, and taxes all over the country. He also began building the *Great Wall* of China to protect his people from invaders from the north. The Great Wall was over 1,500 miles long, 20 feet high, and wide enough for a road along the top.

The Great Wall of China

People disliked paying high taxes. They revolted against the government. New leaders took over. The country grew larger as armies captured more and more land. But to pay for the army, taxes were raised again. The nation grew weak. *Mongol* invaders captured much of northern China.

Buddhism became firmly rooted in China during the third century A.D. Confucianism regained its place of importance.

New leaders gave the Chinese people a better and stronger government. The Mongols were driven back to the lands north of China. Beautiful works of art were created. Books were printed for the first time in the world. Schools improved. China quickly became a better place in which to live.

Many of China's ideas spread to the island nation of *Japan*. The people there changed Chinese ideas to fit their own needs. They started the **Shinto** religion. The nation of Japan was ruled by an emperor with great power and a strong army.

After using many of China's ideas, Japan became uninterested in communicating with other countries. Japan stayed very much to itself for about 600 years. Later, the United States was one of the first nations to trade with Japan.

African Empires Prosper

Muslim *traders* from the Middle East and from North Africa discovered the farming people of West Africa. These Muslims crossed the Sahara to *barter*, or trade.

By about 700, the empire of *Ghana* grew up in West Africa. Using iron tools and weapons, the empire grew. By 1000, it covered over 100,000 square miles.

Arab traders set up their own town near the capital of Ghana. These traders brought wool, copper, and *salt* to trade for gold, ivory, cotton, and slaves.

Ghana's kings made traders pay a *tax* on the goods they brought to Ghana. Traders had to pay more tax on the goods they took home. So much tax was collected to pay for the cost of running the government and for the armies in time of war.

Ghana was a powerful empire until 1087, when it was defeated in war. *Mali* became the second great empire in West Africa. Good *laws* helped Mali prosper.

Arab traders taught Mali about *money* and *credit*. They also brought reading and writing to Mali. In 1324, the *mansa*, or emperor, made a *pilgrimage* to the holy city of *Mecca* in Arabia. The influence of the Arab traders was so great that their *Muslim* religion had now spread to West Africa.

The Mali empire conquered most of what had been Ghana, as well as other lands. Trade made Mali rich, as traders came from as far as Europe seeking gold.

Just as Ghana failed, so did Mali. By 1464, the *Songhai* empire ruled the old Mali lands. The Songhai emperor combined African and Muslim ideas. He divided his nation into *provinces* and chose *governors* to rule them. He kept a full-time army and even had a navy on the Niger River.

In 1591, an army with guns and cannons from *Morocco* in North Africa defeated the Songhais.

Three great African empires had come and gone, but the influence of Muslim Arab traders was never forgotten.

Think About It:

The African empires of Ghana, Mali, and Songhai were once strong. All three failed. How was their failure like the failure of many earlier civilizations?

A Short Review

Decide whether each statement about African empires is true or false. Write "true" or "false" in the space before each statement.

_____   1. Mali was the first West African empire.

_____   2. Most Africans followed the Muslim religion.

_____   3. The mansa was emperor of the Songhai.

_____   4. Salt was an item Arab traders brought to West Africa.

_____   5. A Mali emperor made a religious trip to Mecca.

_____   6. Ghana grew rich from taxing the traders.

_____   7. The Songhai empire fell to an army with guns and cannon.

_____   8. Arab traders used money and credit in Mali.

_____   9. The people of Ghana did not know how to use iron.

_____   10. The empire of Songhai was divided into provinces.

The Americas Have Their Own Civilizations

We've read about great civilizations in Africa, Europe, and Asia. What about North and South America? Civilizations were also developing there.

Three groups of Native Americans had set up empires and were highly civilized. They were the *Aztecs* of Mexico, the *Mayas* of Central America, and the *Incas* of South America.

For years *historians* have felt the Native Americans came from Asia. No matter where they came from, these three groups developed great civilizations.

By about A.D. 100, the Mayas had great city-states. Some of their temples were 200 feet high. These people knew how to use a zero in math before the Europeans did. They had a better calendar than the people of Europe. Their scientists studied astronomy and their doctors knew about surgery.

About the year 1000, the Aztecs from Mexico conquered the Mayas. They controlled many native tribes and made them pay taxes. The Aztecs followed many of the ideas of the Mayas. Their temples, however, were even more beautiful than those of the Mayas.

Montezuma

Montezuma was born in Tenochtitlan, which is the Aztec name for Mexico City. The Aztecs were tough, intelligent people. The ruling class lived in great luxury. Tribute was paid to them by almost 400 conquered towns.

The Aztecs believed in many gods who controlled every part of their lives. To make their gods happy, the Aztec people sacrificed humans to the gods. The Aztecs kept an army just to capture neighboring tribes to use for sacrifice.

The government of the Aztecs was headed by an elected ruler. He was elected by a council from the old ruler's family. Like a god, the ruler had absolute or total control over the Aztec people.

In 1502 Montezuma was elected as ruler. As Montezuma studied to know the gods better, he became concerned. The books told of Quetzalcoatl, one of the Aztec gods. He had been beaten and sent away by the war god. Quetzalcoatl said he would return in a One Reed year to rule the Aztecs again. Many One Reed years passed without Quetzalcoatl returning. The next One Reed year would be in 1519.

The books said Quetzalcoatl would have white skin and a black beard. White skin and beards were unknown to the Aztecs.

When the One Reed year arrived in 1519, the pale-skinned, black-bearded Spanish soldier Hernando Cortés came to Mexico.

Montezuma believed Cortés to be Quetzalcoatl. He knew there would be a battle between Quetzalcoatl and the war god. Montezuma was willing to pay anything to Cortes if he would not come to Tenochtitlan. Cortés, however, set up his camp along the coast and began to

move inland.

Cortés arrived at Tenochtitlan on November 8, 1519. Montezuma greeted him and housed the Spanish troops in the palace. Eventually, Montezuma was made a prisoner of the Spanish. Though Montezuma believed Cortés was the god Quetzalcoatl, many of the people did not. When the Spanish took Montezuma prisoner, the people rebelled. They elected a new leader who would force Quetzalcoatl to leave.

Cortés returned to the coast to make sure things were going well there. He left a large force in Tenochtitlan to keep control of the Aztecs. A battle broke out between the Spanish and the Aztecs. Cortés returned from the coast with a large fighting force. When Montezuma tried to calm his people, they threw stones and arrows at him. Montezuma was badly wounded. The Spanish cared for him, but he died on June 29, 1520. The city he loved so much was totally destroyed in August 1521.

In South America the Incas were also great builders. Their famous Inca Highway was 2,000 miles long. It went through high mountain country and used *suspension bridges* and tunnels. Messages from the ruler to his people were carried by runners along this great highway.

In spite of all the good things these Native Americans did, there were things they did not do. They had gold and silver jewelry, but they didn't have iron weapons. They knew about astronomy, but they didn't use the wheel for transportation. They didn't have horses and cattle. Their civilizations were advanced in some ways and behind in other ways.

Puzzle Quiz

Read each of the following clues and think of a word to fit in the spaces provided. Some spaces have a number under them. At the end of the quiz, there are thirteen numbered spaces. Place the letter from each numbered answer space above the same number in the line at the end of the exercise. The word you spell will tell you what this book is all about. We've given you one letter to get you started on that long word.

1. Another name for the Muslim religion.

   __ __ __ __
     2

2. The Indian tribe that took over the Mayas.

   __ __ __ __
      7

3. A great road-building Indian civilization.

   __ __ __ __
   6 1

4. A Muslim group that lived in Spain.

   __ __ __ __
    11   13

5. A new name for the Eastern Roman Empire.

   __ __ __ __ __ __ __ __
             9 4

6. Muslim name for God.

   __ __ __ __
     5

7. Muslim holy book.

   __ __ __ __
      8

8. Religion started in Japan.

   __ __ __ __ __ __
      10 12

__ __ ^v__ __ __ __ __ __ __ __ __ __ __
1 2 3 4 5 6 7 8 9 10 11 12 13

Europe—Dark Ages and Feudalism

The German tribes that defeated Rome weren't able to set up a strong government. Each tribe had its own leader who set up his own kingdom. The *Franks* formed one of the most important groups. They had become Christians and ruled what is now France. Their most powerful leader was *Charlemagne*, who ruled about A.D. 800. The pope made him protector of the Church and ruler of the *Holy Roman Empire*. As we'll soon see, the Catholic Church became more and more important in the life of the people of Europe.

The 500 years after the Western Roman Empire fell are often called the *Dark Ages*. Less trading was done than before, so few ideas came from other countries. Large farms took the place of cities, and the life of the poor got worse and worse.

If it hadn't been for the Catholic Church, very little of the learning of Greece and Rome would have been saved. Muslim *scholars* had copied these ideas into their language. Now the Catholic Church recopied the ideas of the Greeks and Romans from the Muslims. In addition, the Church ran the only schools. A few wise leaders like Charlemagne wanted education, but most people thought little about learning. They were too busy trying to grow enough to eat.

During this time a way of life called *feudalism* began. In this system, everyone had a definite place. The *king* was at the top. He let rich *noblemen* control large amounts of land. In return, the noblemen became his *vassals*, or servants. They obeyed the king and fought for him in battles against other kings.

Noblemen had their own vassals, too. These men were given land by the nobleman in return for fighting for him. The people in the lowest position were the *serfs*. They were poor farmers who lived on the *manor*, or land owned by a rich person. They spent their lives working for the *lord*, or owner of the manor. Their homes were tiny huts, and their lives were terribly hard. Part of the time they farmed their own fields, and part of the time they farmed for the lord. These serfs never made much of a living and often were killed in battles fighting for the nobleman who owned the land they worked.

But feudalism worked in favor of the serfs and vassals, too. The lord or nobleman expected his vassals to help him. In return, he promised to protect them from other noblemen. To do this, the noblemen built strong *castles* for protection and organized large armies.

> **Think About It:**
> During Europe's Dark Ages, life was hard for most people. Few people had any education. Would education have improved the lives of serfs?

Soldiers in these armies were called *knights*. Only the sons of noblemen could become knights. Serfs and other poor farmers could never expect to wear armor and fight on horseback because each knight had to buy his horse, armor, and weapons. An entirely new way of living was built around the ideas of knighthood. It was called *chivalry*. Knights were expected to be gentlemen and honor the Church.

Boys spent many years training to become knights. They started when they were seven by helping other knights. By the time they were men, they were ready to be knights themselves. One of their favorite sports was the *tournament*, a contest to see who was the best fighter. Knights came from miles around to take part in tournaments. Even using dull swords and blunt lances, a man could still get killed in a tournament.

> **Think About It:**
> If you had lived at the time when feudalism was common, do you think it would have been possible for *you* to have become a knight?

Charlemagne

Charlemagne means "Charles the Great." Charlemagne was the greatest military leader of the Middle Ages. He made the Church more powerful and built the greatest empire since Rome.

Charlemagne was born in 742 in what is now northern France. His father was called Pepin the Short and was king of the Franks. After his father and brother died, Charlemagne became king of the Franks in 771.

The Franks and the Saxons did not get along well. When the Saxons killed a missionary and some Franks, Charlemagne rode with his army to punish them. He forced the Saxons to become Christians.

The pope asked for help when the Lombards from Germany invaded Italy. Charlemagne defeated them and added their lands to his empire.

One of his few defeats came in Spain in 778. His nephew, Roland, died in that battle.

Charlemagne built churches all over his kingdom. When the Saxons revolted in 782, they burned many of these churches. In fury, Charlemagne killed over 4,500 Saxon leaders.

Charlemagne started a school for both the rich and the poor. He felt religion and education were important.

When his son Pepin joined a plot against Charlemagne, Pepin was sent to live in a monastery.

On Christmas Day, 800, the pope crowned Charlemagne emperor. This was a reward for helping the pope defeat his enemies.

Charlemagne tried to help all the people in his empire, including the poor. When he forgave his son and asked him to return home, Pepin chose to stay at the monastery.

Charlemagne's only other living son was Louis. After an accident hurt Charlemagne, he crowned Louis as king. In 814 Charlemagne died and was buried sitting on his marble throne.

Middle Ages

All of the things pictured below and on page 50 were important to knights in the Middle Ages.

Armor—Metal plates, or sheets, were worn over a suit made of tiny linked chains to further protect important parts of the body.

Chain mail—This body armor was made of hundreds of interlocking metal rings. It was fairly light in weight and let the wearer bend, turn, or twist.

Crossbow—In 1139, Pope Innocent II declared the crossbow unfit for Christians to fight with, but King Richard encouraged its use in the Third Crusade. The crossbow could shoot an arrow up to 400 yards with force enough to go through various kinds of armor.

Pike—This was used by both foot soldiers and armored knights to pierce armor, and hook, trip, and cut.

Suit of Armor—Good armor had to be specially made for the person who was to wear it. The armor shown on page 43 would weigh about 50 pounds.

Sword—These two-handed swords could knock a knight out of the saddle or off his horse, unless he was firmly seated. They would even cut through armor.

Tournament—These friendly contests determined which knights were the best fighters. In the picture shown, the knights are trying to knock each other off their horses. The tournament became a social occasion, like a fair or carnival with sideshows. People came from miles around for the event. Today, we still have contests called "tournaments" to see who is best in golf, tennis, and other sports.

Shield—The shield was very important for a knight going into battle. It protected him from his enemies. It also let the other knights know who he was so his friends wouldn't hurt him by mistake.

Shield

A design on the shield couldn't be copied by any other family. Each thing on the shield means something. For example, the shape of the shield above was used in the 1400's. The cross in the upper right-hand corner shows that the knight who carried this shield may have gone on a Crusade. The battle-axe may have been one of his weapons in that Crusade.

Armor—for the body; front and back buckled or strapped together

Tournament

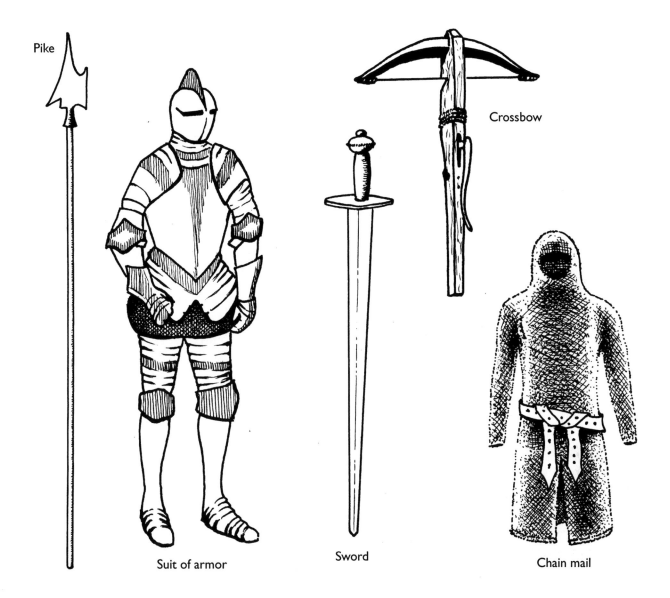

Pike

Crossbow

Suit of armor

Sword

Chain mail

The Church Grows More Powerful

As the Church became stronger, it made several laws. One such law made it wrong to have battles over the weekend or on holy days. Another important rule made it against the law to hurt religious workers or farmers. This rule helped the poor of Europe.

The Catholic Church's leader, the *pope*, became as powerful as a king. He owned land for the Church and was the only person who could appoint a *priest* or *bishop*. Since religion was so important to the people, this gave the pope great power. If people didn't follow the rules of the Church, the pope could force them to leave the Roman Catholic Church.

During this time many religious men became *monks*. These men lived in *monasteries*. No one was supposed to hurt people in a monastery. Monasteries became safe places for travelers and townspeople in time of war. Also, monasteries became places for learning. The monks copied books with Greek and

Roman ideas. Usually monks were the best-educated people in the area.

The Muslims had long ago captured the land of Palestine, where Christ was born. In 1095, the Church started the first religious war to win back the **Holy Land** (Palestine) from the Muslims. These religious wars were called **Crusades**. During the next 200 years, a total of eight Crusades were fought in the Holy Land. Noblemen and kings raised great armies and left their homes to fight the Muslims in the Holy Land.

The First Crusade was able to take the Holy Land away from the Muslims. Fifty years later the Muslims recaptured much of this land. Even though seven Crusades followed, the Muslims were able to keep control of the Holy Land. The Fourth Crusade ended up fighting the people of Constantinople, which was the center of the Orthodox Church (the eastern branch of the Catholic Church), rather than the Muslims!

Think About It:
People of one culture can learn a lot from those of other cultures. How is it possible for nations to learn and improve as a result of something like the Crusades?

As a military idea, the Crusades were a terrible failure. But in other ways, they did a lot for Europe. Noblemen became less powerful. Kings had a better chance to **unite** a country under one ruler. New ideas borrowed from the Muslims were brought back to Europe. When the people of Europe saw some of the things the Muslims had, they wanted them too. Trade became more important. Cities in Italy, such as Venice and Genoa, became important ports and centers of trade.

Though it cost thousands of lives to do so, Europe had come gradually out of the Dark Ages. Once again, a religious war had changed civilization.

Think About It:
What were some of the ways the Catholic Church had great power over the people of Europe during this time in history?

The Middle Ages

Answer each of the following sets of questions using the map on page 46. We've given you answers to choose from. You may use any choice more than once.

Cities:

Choose from Rome, Constantinople, Jerusalem.

1. What city is the center of Eastern Christendom?   _____

2. What city is the center of Latin Christendom?   _____

3. This is a holy city for Christianity, Judaism, and Islam, but on the map, the followers of Islam hold the city.   _____

Empires:

Choose from Byzantine, Muslim, Latin Christendom.

1. This empire controls land south of the   _____
   Mediterranean Sea.

2. This empire lies between the Black Sea   _____
   and the Mediterranean Sea.

Religions:

Choose from Roman Catholicism, Eastern Orthodox, Islam.

1. The Byzantine Empire is of this religion.   _____

2. The Muslim Empire is of this religion.   _____

3. Most of Europe practices this religion.   _____

Continents:

Choose from Europe, Asia, Africa.

1. On what continent is Latin Christendom   _____
   shown?

2. On which two continents is the Eastern   _____
   Orthodox religion to be found?

3. On what continent is Islam shown?   _____

Crusades:

Choose from Jerusalem, Constantinople, Islam, Roman Catholicism.

1. The Crusaders passed through this city   _____
   to reach the Muslims.

2. This holy city was the goal of the First   _____
   Crusade.

3. People of this religion were fighting the   _____
   Muslims.

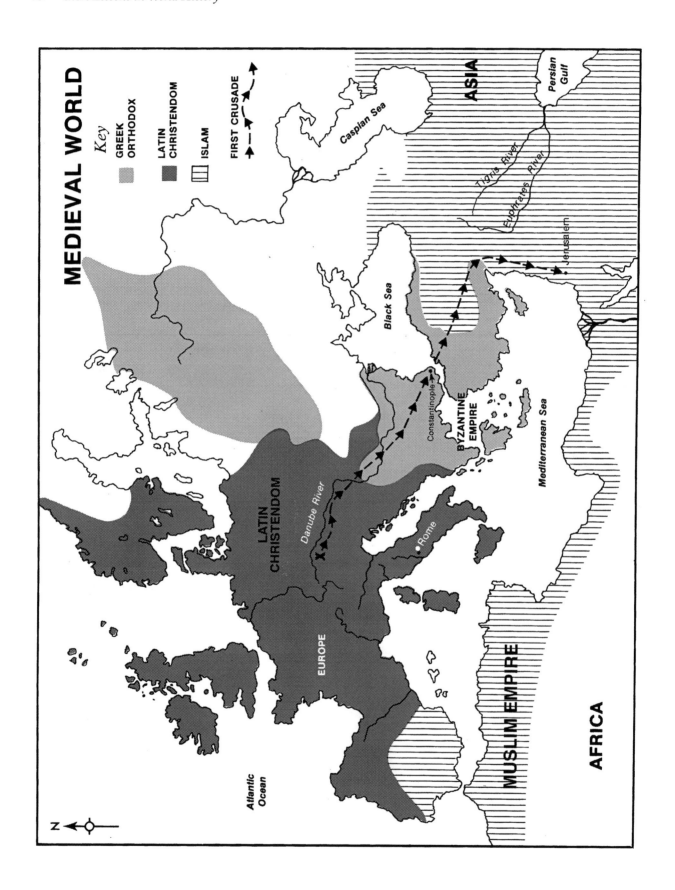

LATER MIDDLE AGES

Introduction

The second half of the *Middle Ages* was a time of many changes. Towns, cities, and trade again began to thrive in Europe. The trade between Europe and the rest of the world became more important than it had ever been before. Learning, too, again came alive. As more and more changes occurred, the nations of England and France gained in power.

In many ways, this was a time of putting civilization back together as it was before the barbarian invasions and the Dark Ages.

Europe was to become increasingly involved with two very different continents: Asia and Africa. Let's take a brief look at what was happening there.

The World Changes in Asia and Africa

As you remember, China was taken over by the fierce *Mongol* invaders. Led by *Genghis Khan* and his grandson, *Kublai Khan,* these wild horsemen captured land as far west as the Byzantine Empire. In fact, the Mongols put together the largest empire the world has ever known.

These horsemen rode from one side of Russia to the other. They built good roads and used a Pony Express system for carrying messages. Their traders went all over the world. Their entire empire used *paper money,*

which was something Europe hadn't considered. They knew how to use the *magnetic compass* and *gunpowder.* Their horsemen used stirrups to steady the rider. All these ideas they gave to Europe. And Europe put these ideas to uses that changed its history.

After the Mongols lost control of most of their empire, they took over India. These *Moguls,* as they were called, allowed people to follow the religion they preferred but set up one government for the entire nation.

During the 200 years of Mogul rule, Indian artists created many great works of art and architecture. One example is the *Taj Mahal.* The Taj Mahal is a beautiful tomb built by one of the Mogul rulers. Its beauty is so great that tourists still travel from all over the world to see it.

The Crusaders' capture of Constantinople was the beginning of the end for the Byzantine Empire. Even though the empire got back some power, its strong days were over. By 1453 the *Turks* ended the empire when they captured Constantinople. The last area of the empire became part of what is now Turkey and Russia. The Eastern Roman Empire was gone!

Several very powerful nations had come and gone in Africa by this time. Such names as *Cush, Aksum,* and *Songhai* were important for a time and then forgotten. Other names like *Mali* and *Ghana* were important a thousand years ago and have again become important today.

Think About It:
Russian Cossacks have been known for years as wild fighters and great horsemen. Did you read anything in the last couple of pages that might give you some idea why the Cossacks are this way?

The End of Feudalism in Europe

Returning Crusaders brought with them new things and new ideas. The people of Europe saw fine silks and tasted wonderful *spices*. The silks were beautiful, and the spices helped improve the taste of their food. More of these things were demanded! Soon, European traders were sailing from the *seaports* of Venice and Genoa in Italy. They crossed the Mediterranean Sea and met Arab traders in Syria and Egypt.

So began an influential group of people called *merchants*, or businesspeople. These traders brought their goods directly to the people. Since roads were so bad, many things were shipped by boat on rivers. Towns began along rivers or in harbors where traders' boats stopped. Other towns grew up around castles, which had protected the people for many years.

Slowly at first, then faster and faster, people left the feudal manors and moved into the new towns. No longer were serfs content to spend their lives working on a nobleman's farm. They wanted land of their own, or even a business.

Think About It:
In Europe bubonic plague struck. It was called the Black Death. Between 1347 and 1350, more than one-fourth of all the people in Europe died. How did this loss of population help to end feudalism?

In order to be truly free from noblemen, people in a town would buy the town's land from the lord. In return for money, the lord gave the town a *charter*, or a paper making the townsfolk free.

The lords and noblemen still had great power, though. They charged a *toll*, or fee, for traders and travelers crossing their land or passing by their castles. This toll made many lords rich, but it also helped end feudalism for good. As the traders and merchants become more important, they protested these tolls. When a king tried to unite a country, the merchants were likely to be in favor of him if he promised certain powers or privileges to the merchants. Once a king ruled a land, no more tolls were paid to lords. This helped trade, and trade in turn helped the new nation grow.

This time in Europe's history also saw *banking* become important. Each trader brought money with him from a different place. The value of money was different from country to country. Moneychangers worked with the merchants to decide how much each kind of money was worth. There was always the danger of thieves taking a merchant's money. Soon the merchants began to pay the moneychangers to keep their money and protect it. Then it was just a short step to loaning money to merchants. In that way, banks began.

Another aid to trade was the *Hanseatic League*. This organization helped merchants trade safely among countries.

Something else was beginning in the new towns. This was a *guild*, an organization somewhat like today's labor unions. A guild made sure its members did a good job and charged a fair price for their work. It also set up a system for training new workers. A member of the carpenters' guild, for example, might decide he needed help. He would agree to feed and clothe a boy who wanted to learn to be a carpenter. This boy was an *apprentice*, or beginning worker. When he had learned to do a carpenter's work, he began to receive pay for his work. Later he might even set up his own business.

As merchants, bankers, and guild members became better off, they formed a new class of people. This was the *middle class.* Before this time, the lords had been the upper class, and the serfs were the lower class. Now this new class of townspeople was becoming very important in the life of Europe. —

Think About It:

The ending of feudalism caused many changes. The middle class developed. How did having a middle class help towns and trade to grow?

Kings and Nations Gain Power

Except for Charlemagne, most European kings had been weak under feudalism. With the growth of trade and towns, this weakness would change. In 1492 two great Spanish rulers, *Ferdinand* and *Isabella*, were able to bring Spain under the control of one ruling family. It was this ruling family that finally forced the Muslims out of Spain and started to support the exploration of new trade routes.

Two other great nations were each getting themselves united under one king. One of these was *England*, or Britain. After the Romans left Britain, *barbarian* tribes of *Angles, Saxons*, and *Jutes* took control. Years later, such leaders as *Alfred the Great* and the legendary *King Arthur* did much to unite the country against further barbarian attacks.

France was the other strong European nation at this time. The king of France was trying to control the lords so he could have a united France. In 1066, a Frenchman, *William the Conqueror,* crossed the English Channel with his troops and defeated the English. William became the first king of a united England. The rulers of both England and France began to grow more and more powerful.

In 1215, the king of England was so cruel that the noblemen refused to obey him. They forced the king to sign the famous *Magna Carta*, which was the beginning of freedom for the English people. It protected the people from unjust government. The *Bill of Rights*, written in America 500 years later, is much like the Magna Carta. In fact, many laws today are based on English legal ideas of this period.

Another good idea from England was the *Parliament.* People were elected to go to Parliament to pass laws and help the king with government. This prevented the king from becoming too powerful and forgetting the ideas of the people. The U.S. *Congress* today is much the same.

French kings continued to gain power. One reason was the growth of towns and trade. People who lived in towns were free. They didn't have to spend their lives working for a nobleman. But they did need the protection a king could provide. A king could also require all the cities in a nation to use the same money and speak the same language. This helped trade.

The king collected taxes from many towns and villages. This gave him money to hire soldiers for his own army. He no longer depended upon the lords and noblemen to help him. The people were safer with the hired army. The king kept it all the time, not just when the country was at war.

Think About It:

Kings gained power as feudalism ended. Why was a strong king needed in order to have a strong nation?

Strangely enough, a Chinese invention brought the final end to feudalism. *Gunpowder* made it possible to destroy castles and knights in armor. No longer was a lord's castle a place of great safety. Only by working together as a nation and having a large army could the people be well protected.

Feudalism had ended. The great nations of Spain, England, and France were controlled by strong kings. Trade was important. Europe was ready to become great.

Learning Begins Again in Europe

After over 500 years of the Dark Ages, learning again prospered in Europe. Books in Greek and Arabic were *translated* into Latin so educated Europeans could study them. Such great thinkers as Aristotle again became known and studied.

Among the great teachers and *scholars* of this time was *Thomas Aquinas.* His writings were read by most of the educated people in Europe. Even today, his works are widely studied.

Colleges and *universities* began to appear all over Europe. Parents who wanted their sons to become teachers, doctors, lawyers, priests, or high government officials sent them to college. With more education, they were better able to do their jobs. As a result, nations became stronger as better-educated people helped run them.

During this time the people of Europe finally learned to use *Arabic numerals* and the *zero. Roman numerals* were hard to use and had no zero. Without the zero, mathematics was slow and difficult. The Greeks' ideas for geometry and algebra were finally taught in Europe at this time, too.

The beginnings of modern science came as well. Chemistry got its start. The first scientists began their work. The *scientific method* of finding facts by observation also began. This is the method used today in scientific experiments.

Important books, poems, and music were written. A German named Gutenberg invented *movable type* for use with a printing press. Letters could be used over and over on many pages. No longer did a whole page have to be carved on a block of wood. Hundreds of books could be printed in a short time. As a result, the written word could be read by thousands instead of dozens.

Many churches were built during these years. It wasn't uncommon for all the people in a town or city to join together to build a beautiful church. Some of these great churches took two or three lifetimes to finish. New and better kinds of *architecture* were used.

The life of the people of Europe centered around the Catholic Church. Educated men were needed to make the Church stronger. The Church began to send out *friars* to act as teachers. These were the first *missionaries*, even though many of them ended up as college teachers. Their job was to educate the people and get them interested in the Church.

Think About It:

The Church was very important in the Middle Ages. How did a strong church help to spread learning and unite people?

The Renaissance and the Reformation

As the Middle Ages came to an end, Europe was changing rapidly. A new age called the *Renaissance* was beginning. The Renaissance was a time when art and architecture were at their finest.

During this time some of the world's greatest paintings were created. Such famous Italian painters as *Leonardo da Vinci*, *Raphael*, *Titian*, and *Michelangelo* lived and painted during this time. Many of their best works weren't painted on canvas but on the walls and ceilings of great churches.

Beautiful carvings or sculptures were also produced. Michelangelo was an all-around great artist. Not only did he paint, he also created sculptures and designed grand buildings. Architects during the Renaissance used ideas from Greece and Rome to build their palaces and churches.

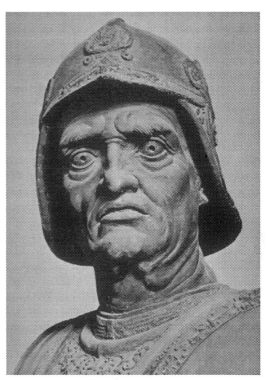

Da Vinci sculpture

Joan of Arc

Joan was born in 1412 in France. She had her first vision when she was 12. For the next four years, Joan had more visions. The Archangel Michael and Saint Catherine and Saint Margaret told Joan to leave her home and serve her king.

Charles VII should have been king but wasn't, since England ruled France. The voices Joan heard said she would help make Charles the king. She would also drive the English out of France.

In May 1428, Joan went to the captain of the fort of Vaucouleurs. She asked for soldiers. The captain refused. She returned in January and stayed at the fort. By now people remembered an old prophecy. It said France would be saved by a maid, or young girl.

On February 12, Joan went to the captain and told him the soldiers of Charles had lost a battle. When the captain finally got news of the battle, he took Joan to a priest, whom she asked for a blessing. This proved she was not a witch.

Joan was given six soldiers. She cut her hair short and dressed as a man. Then she rode to meet Charles. She told the priests who met her she would defeat the English at Orléans. Then she would take Charles to Reims to be crowned king.

She convinced Charles she could do what she claimed. However, religious leaders asked if she came from God or from the devil.

Dressed in white armor and with a sword found buried near a church, Joan set out on April 27, 1429. She led her army toward Orléans.

Joan and her army had to enter Orléans by crossing a river. The English held forts on either side. A strong wind kept Joan's forces from crossing. Suddenly, the wind died down. Joan and her army entered Orléans.

The French people wanted to fight the English. Their leaders refused. The English said Joan was a witch and they would burn her if they caught her.

Joan led an attack on an English fort. The French were driven back. Joan called on her soldiers to attack again, and this time they took the fort. Two more forts were taken in the next two days. The French wanted to stop, but Joan said to go on.

During the next battle, Joan was wounded. Even so, the French won, and the siege of Orléans was over.

Joan predicted she would live one year. On June 11, she was again injured in battle. Even so, she led her troops to victory. On July 16, 1429, Joan and Charles VII entered Reims. Charles was crowned king of France.

Joan led a small army to Paris, even though Charles held back. She attacked on September 8, a holy day. The attack failed and Joan was hit by an arrow in the leg.

In early 1430, Charles signed treaties with the English. Most troops stopped fighting—but not Joan. In May, she was defeated in battle and did not get back to the city before the gates closed. English soldiers captured her.

King Charles did not try to help. Joan was tried by 50 church officials in February 1431. The court proved no crimes. Joan became ill and was chained to her bed. She was threatened with torture if she did not confess to crimes against God.

On May 30, Joan was taken to the market square. There she was tied to a stake and burned to death. Her ashes were thrown into the river.

In 1456, a new trial was held. Joan was found innocent 25 years after her death.

Nearly all the great art of the Renaissance dealt with religion. Most artists painted Mary and Jesus. Religious people were often the subject of statues. The finest buildings were churches. Even the best music was likely to be church music.

The power of the Catholic Church did not continue, however. In 1517, *Martin Luther* started a movement that affected the great power of the Church.

Martin Luther was a monk who felt the Catholic Church had some problems. Luther felt it was wrong for the Church to allow men to buy church jobs. He also felt it was wrong for people to buy forgiveness for their sins. He demanded that the Church stop such practices. When the Church leaders didn't listen to him, he took action. In 1517, he nailed a list of his protests to the door of a church. As punishment, Luther was *excommunicated*, or expelled, from the Catholic Church four years later. But damage had been done to the Church. In those four years, many people had listened to and agreed with the ideas of Martin Luther. They thought the Catholic Church should be reformed. These ideas became part of the *Reformation*.

The total power of the Catholic Church was broken. The people who agreed with Luther's protests were called *Protestants*. Their ideas quickly spread over Europe. The changes they made in the Church started a new branch of the Christian religion. In time, dozens of branches of the Protestant Church appeared.

True-False Puzzle

Answer each of the following statements by writing "true" or "false" on the line before it. Circle the letter from the group of letters below that matches the number of the statement and the answer. For example, if the answer to question 1 is true, circle the "R" after "True" and above number 1. Do the same for all eleven questions.

True	R	E	F	C	S	M	E	N	I	I	R
False	J	A	G	O	R	N	A	T	O	O	N
	1	2	3	4	5	6	7	8	9	10	11

_____ 1. Kublai Khan was a Mongol.

_____ 2. Alfred the Great was a king of England.

_____ 3. Many great paintings came out of the Renaissance.

_____ 4. Martin Luther was not punished by the Catholic Church.

_____ 5. Roman numerals include a zero.

_____ 6. Towns became important in the later Middle Ages.

_____ 7. Gunpowder was first used in Europe.

_____ 8. Protestants were not Christians.

_____ 9. Education was important during the late Middle Ages.

_____ 10. Thomas Aquinas was from China.

_____ 11. Churches were no longer important after the Reformation.

Now look at the letters you circled. If your answers are correct, the circled letters (read from left to right) will spell out a word that became important at the end of the Middle Ages. Write that word on the line below.

_____

Puzzle Quiz

Read the following clues. Think of a word that matches the clue and place it in the row or column that has the same number as the number of the clue. The answers were taken from the words in bold italics in the pages you recently read.

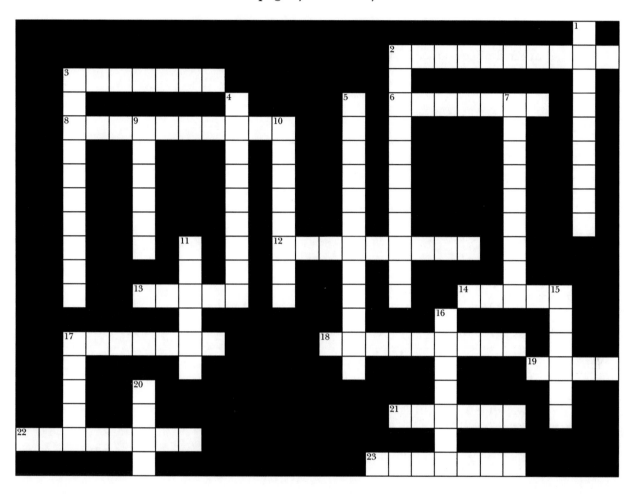

Across

2. This chapter has been about the later _____ _____.

3. Thomas _____ was one of Europe's greatest teachers.

6. Leonardo _____ _____ was a great Renaissance painter from Italy.

8. What English lawmaking body is much like the U.S. Congress?

12. What league or organization helped trade?

13. What was an organized group of workers called who all did the same kind of work?

14. What people captured Constantinople in 1453?

Across *(continued)*

17. What was the name of the paper that made the people of a town free?

18. What is another name for "businesspeople"?

19. What is another word for a fee paid to cross another's property?

21. What are churchmen who are sent out to teach called?

22. What kind of coastal cities were Venice and Genoa in Italy?

23. Genghis and Kublai Khan were from what group of people?

Down

1. What was the name of the highly structured kind of living that ended during the later Middle Ages?

2. What class of people appeared after towns became important?

3. What name described a boy who was learning a trade by working with a skilled worker?

4. Who was Queen Isabella's husband?

5. What were the places to which boys and men went to learn?

7. In 1066, William the _____ captured Britain for France.

9. The Hanseatic _____ helped merchants trade safely.

10. What beautiful building was built by a Mogul ruler in India?

11. What was one of the things used for cooking that the people of Europe wanted from the Eastern world?

15. What was the name of one of the tribes that took over England after the Romans left?

16. What business grew from moneychanging?

17. The Magna _____ gave certain rights to English people.

20. What numeral used by the Arabs was used by the people of Europe near the end of the Middle Ages?

EUROPE'S POWER GROWS GREATER

Introduction

The years after the Middle Ages brought great change in Europe. European explorers arrived in unknown lands across the Atlantic Ocean. They called them the *Americas*. New nations were formed in Europe. Other nations seemed to be at war with each other most of the time.

Several great *revolutions* were fought and won during this time. The *New World* across the sea was on its way to becoming important in world affairs.

A New World Is Explored

Several things happened at just the right time to lead to the exploration of the New World. Let's take just a minute to review these things.

The Crusades had caused an increase in trade between Europe and the nations of the *Far East*. Along with this, *Marco Polo's* book about his travels to China had been read all over Europe.

Marco Polo found an ancient civilization in China. The teachings of *Confucius* encouraged learning and respect. The Chinese had a strong central government and families that worked together. *Dynasties* of rulers for centuries had unified the nation.

The Chinese invented paper, had a civil service system for choosing government officials, and were interested in the arts. Fine pottery, carved jade, and good poetry represented national feelings.

Marco Polo found the Chinese used paper money, had a mail service, and transported goods on the 1,000-mile-long Grand Canal. The emperor, *Kublai Khan*, had a beautiful palace and room for 6,000 guests. This was amazing because *Genghis Khan*, his grandfather, had led an army of Mongol raiders to conquer part of China just a generation earlier.

Korea was much like China. Confucius was studied, as was *Buddhism*, which the Chinese took to Korea. Though most Koreans were farmers, the people had a system of writing, could print books, and eventually invented movable type.

China's influence was also felt in *Japan*. Buddhism was popular, and many Japanese wrote with Chinese *characters*.

Japan had an emperor, but the real power was held by nobles. Fighting men called *samurai* were much like the knights of the Middle Ages. A military leader called a *shogun* was the country's most powerful leader.

The year before Marco Polo came, the Chinese attacked Japan. A storm saved the Japanese by destroying the Chinese ships. Six years later another storm stopped a second Chinese attack. Japan was saved by what its people called a "divine wind."

Marco Polo's travels caused great interest in Europe. Chinese inventions and goods were welcomed. Especially valuable was China's magnetic compass, which had a needle that always pointed north. With the compass, for the first time European sailors could sail out of sight of land and be sure of their direction.

Even more important for expanding trade had been the growth of trading cities, such as Genoa and Venice in Italy. These cities lay on the trade route of most goods coming across the Mediterranean Sea. Other nations such as Spain and Portugal felt left out. They wanted to find a *water route* to China so their ships could sail there and back without using expensive *caravans* across land. Spain had just been united under one family. Conditions in 1492 were right for *Christopher Columbus* to set sail.

When Columbus landed in the New World, he thought he was just where he wanted to be, the *East Indies*. If Columbus could have studied Viking history, he might have known where he really was. He was far from the East Indies, and he had not reached a "new" land. *Viking* sailors had landed in what is now Canada about 500 years before Columbus set sail, but Columbus didn't know that.

Most people were sure Columbus had reached an unknown land. A race to control that land began. Explorers from half a dozen nations sailed to the New World. Each one claimed what he saw for his own nation. England, France, the Netherlands, Spain, and Sweden claimed land in North America. Spain and Portugal claimed South America.

Portugal and Spain were the world leaders in sailing ventures. In 1497, *Vasco da Gama* sailed around Africa and into the Indian Ocean. From 1519 to 1522, *Ferdinand Magellan's* tiny fleet of ships sailed around the world and back to Spain.

Because of the great number of Spanish explorers, that nation was ahead of the other nations in claiming land in the New World. Spain did not treat the people of these new lands well, however. *Hernando Cortés* was destroying the great Aztec civilization at the same time Magellan was sailing around the world. Ten years later, *Francisco Pizarro* was torturing Incas in South America in order to find their great treasures.

Even though these and other Spanish *expeditions* had Catholic priests with them, they often mistreated the natives they met. Killing Native Americans to make them accept Christianity was common. Making slaves of them and making them work in the gold mines were even more common.

When the English began to send settlers to the New World in 1607, they treated the natives a little better than the Spaniards had done. But, only the French who settled in Canada were kind to the Native Americans.

> **Think About It:**
> The desire to trade created an interest in exploration. Explorers found new lands to settle. How did these changes sometimes cause suffering to people in Europe as well as in the new lands?

The large nations interested in the same new lands soon began to argue about who should control the land. In 1588, the Spaniards sent a great fleet of ships to destroy England. England's *Sir Francis Drake* met this great *Armada* and helped to defeat it. Stormy weather then destroyed most of the rest of the Armada. This was the beginning of the end of Spain's great power.

European nations continued to fight, however. Parts of nations fought other parts of the same nation. *Colonies* in the New World got into the fights as well. Today's friend was likely to be tomorrow's enemy.

Think About It:

Why can it be said that if Columbus hadn't sailed when he did, someone else would have taken his place within a few years?

Ships Used in Exploration

The Arab *dhow* (at the top of the next page) was a small coasting vessel used by Muslim sailors in the Mediterranean Sea. It had sails that were almost triangular. These sails could be moved to catch the lightest breeze. Because of their sails, these ships could sail into the wind or even against the wind and still move forward!

The Portuguese *caravel* (at the bottom of the next page) was a ship similar to the one Columbus used to sail to the New World in 1492. This ship used the triangular sail of the Arabs only on the mizzenmast (the mast on the back of the ship). The other two sails—the foresail and the mainsail—were square.

Soon the caravel wasn't used anymore because it didn't go fast enough. Like the caravel, the new ships had three masts. However, they had five sails instead of three. The five sails helped the ships to go to the New World faster than three sails could.

European Colonies in the New World

The map on page 61 shows the land European countries claimed in the New World. These new colonies became part of the European nations' world empires. Study the map, then try to answer the questions. Underline the correct answers.

1. The two continents regarded as the New World were:

   a) Europe and Africa   c) South America and North America

   b) North America and Africa   d) Europe and North America

2. The ocean the Europeans had to cross to get to the New World was the:

   a) Atlantic Ocean   b) Pacific Ocean   c) Arctic Ocean

3. The continent on which Spain, England, France, and Portugal are located is:

   a) Africa   b) North America   c) South America   d) Europe

4. This European country claimed the biggest chunk of land in the New World:

   a) England   b) France   c) Spain   d) Portugal

5. This European country claimed land north and south of the equator:

   a) England   b) France   c) Spain   d) Portugal

(Continues on page 62)

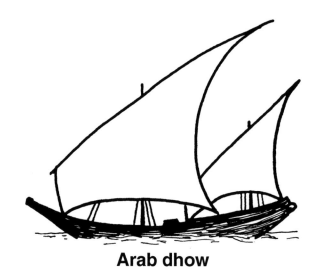

Arab dhow

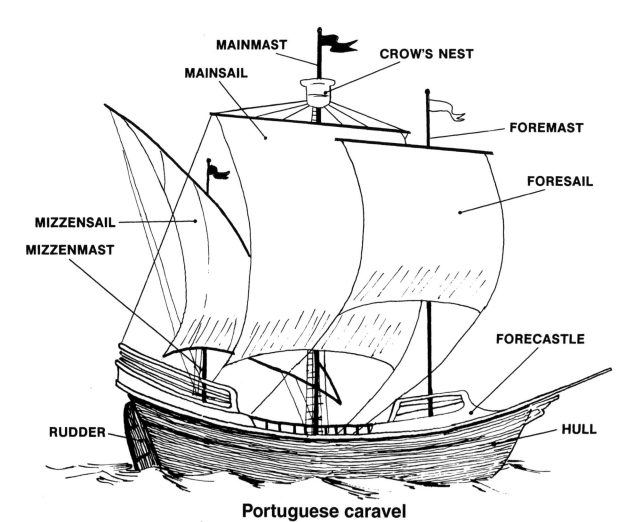

MAINMAST

CROW'S NEST

MAINSAIL

FOREMAST

FORESAIL

MIZZENSAIL

MIZZENMAST

FORECASTLE

RUDDER

HULL

Portuguese caravel

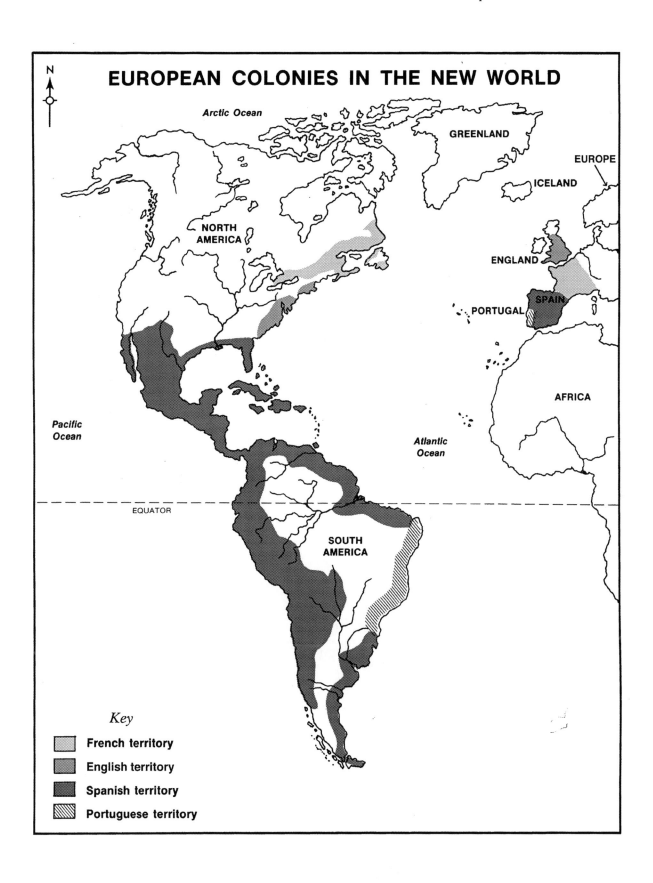

EUROPEAN COLONIES IN THE NEW WORLD

Arctic Ocean

GREENLAND

EUROPE

ICELAND

NORTH AMERICA

ENGLAND

SPAIN

PORTUGAL

Pacific Ocean

AFRICA

Atlantic Ocean

EQUATOR

SOUTH AMERICA

Key

French territory

English territory

Spanish territory

Portuguese territory

6. This country claimed land only in South America:

    a) England b) France c) Spain d) Portugal

7. This country claimed land in the New World that touched both the Atlantic and Pacific oceans:

    a) England b) France c) Spain d) Portugal

8. The land farthest north was claimed by:

    a) England b) France c) Spain d) Portugal

9. Most of the east coast of North America was in the possession of:

    a) England b) France c) Spain d) Portugal

10. The largest island shown east of North America and west of Europe is:

    a) Greenland b) Iceland

Europe—A Continent at War

The years after the English victory over the Spanish Armada brought continued fighting. Because of the defeat of the Armada, Spain had gone from one of the world's most powerful nations to a fairly weak one. England and France both tried to gain more power. Several countries had *civil wars* in which one part of the country fought another part. Many of these civil wars were over religion—Protestants fought Catholics. Wars were also fought because one nation thought another nation was becoming too strong. Several new nations appeared. For about 200 years, Europe was in a state of confusion.

During this time many of Europe's *royal families* became powerful. Members of royal families were the rulers of nations. Often one royal family would go to war with another family that had tried to lessen its power. Many royal families made their nations go to war because of religion. For example, the *Hapsburg* family in Spain and Austria was Catholic.

Several times Hapsburgs were involved in wars with Protestants. One religious war that Austria fought lasted 30 years! The war left Austria weaker than it had been and resulted in freedom for many small German states.

For many years France allowed people of all religions to live together in peace. Across the English Channel in England, the *Tudor family* was usually Protestant. Most of the English followed their ruler's religion.

This led to problems, though. People who didn't follow the ruler's religion had great troubles. Plymouth Colony in the New World was started by people who weren't welcome in England because their religion was different from the ruler's religion.

When England wasn't having religious problems, it was having government problems! Some civil wars were fought over the question of power. English kings believed in the **divine right** of kings. However, most people felt that God hadn't given kings such power. They felt the **Parliament**, which was elected by the people, had the right to make laws. Who was right? Did the king have all the power, or did Parliament share that power with the king? A **revolution** decided this issue. The English people got a **Bill of Rights**, which helped protect them from the unjust rule of kings. They also got a **prime minister**, who was made leader in Parliament to help pass laws for the people. These changes greatly weakened the power of the English monarchy.

In other countries royal families were still strong. The ruling **Bourbon family** became very powerful in France. **King Louis XIV** of France ruled for 72 years. He believed in the divine right of kings. He also believed all French people should be Catholics. Many people who weren't Catholic left France. Some of these people moved to the New World and settled in Canada.

A courtyard at Versailles

The kings who followed Louis XIV tried to gain total control over the people. Such rulers are called **despots**. Misuse of such power can cause serious troubles.

Like the French kings, the Hapsburgs who ruled Austria became despots. Some Austrian rulers freed the serfs of the country. Such kind despots were called **benevolent despots**. A benevolent despot ruled strongly but for the good of the people.

Prussia, the nation north of Austria, was quickly becoming the most warlike of the German states. Its most famous ruler, **Frederick the Great**, was a benevolent despot. He didn't free the serfs, but he did build schools and allow religious freedom. He also gained much land for Prussia in war.

Russia was another land that still had serfs, even though feudalism had ended in most of Europe years before. In Russia the ruler was called a **czar**. Not only did the early czars keep serfs, they also forced other poor people to become serfs. These Russian despots weren't benevolent. Some czars, like **Peter the Great** and **Catherine the Great**, did try to make things better for their people. They tried to make good ideas from other parts of the world work in Russia. Even so, they kept complete power for themselves. After many years Russia finally gave freedom to its serfs. But even after they were free, the Russian serfs still had a hard life.

Think About It:
Strong rulers help make nations strong. Why did citizens of some powerful nations object to their strong leaders?

Catherine the Great

A girl named Sophia was born in Prussia in 1729. Her parents were Germans of noble birth but without money. Fourteen years later word came that Grand Duke Peter of Russia was interested in Sophia as a future bride.

Sophia traveled to Russia, where a sleigh pulled by three horses carried her through the bitter cold to St. Petersburg. Two years later, Sophia married Peter and became Grand Duchess Catherine.

Peter was insane, but even so, his mother, Empress Elizabeth, wanted him to rule Russia one day. When Empress Elizabeth died on Christmas Day, 1761, Peter took the throne.

Peter angered the Church. He hurt trade and foreign relations and was hated by his people. Catherine, who was once called Sophia, was liked by the people. She learned Russian and planned to take over the throne.

Army leaders helped Catherine. When Peter took a trip, Catherine took control. She became Empress of Russia. Nine days later her husband was dead. A military leader probably killed him. Catherine said she knew nothing about the murder.

Catherine set out to make Russia stronger. She built up foreign trade and strengthened the army and navy. Ports on the Black Sea and Baltic Sea were opened. New cities were built. Catherine provided better education and helped women have better lives.

Catherine did not help the serfs. These poor workers were not much better off than slaves. When they asked for better treatment, Catherine crushed their revolts.

Her son Paul was not among Catherine's favorites. Later she gave her love to her grandson, Alexander. Catherine also gave expensive presents to the many men she liked.

For 34 years this German woman ruled Russia. On November 10, 1796, she died of a stroke and Paul became emperor. Perhaps her habit of using a pound of coffee a day to make six cups of coffee shortened her life.

Catherine was a strong ruler who helped Russia modernize and grow. She wasn't always a nice person.

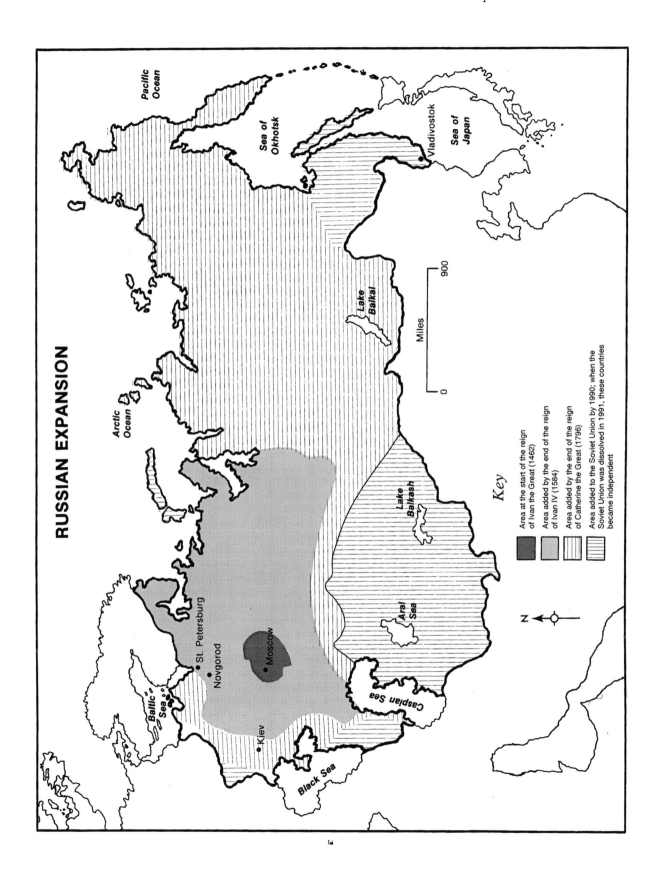

RUSSIAN EXPANSION

Pacific Ocean

Sea of Okhotsk

Vladivostok

Sea of Japan

Lake Baikal

Miles

900

0

Arctic Ocean

Lake Balkash

Aral Sea

Key

N

St. Petersburg

Novgorod

Moscow

Kiev

Baltic Sea

Caspian Sea

Black Sea

Area at the start of the reign of Ivan the Great (1462)

Area added by the end of the reign of Ivan IV (1584)

Area added by the end of the reign of Catherine the Great (1796)

Area added to the Soviet Union by 1990; when the Soviet Union was dissolved in 1991, these countries became independent

Russia Questions

The map "Russian Expansion" on page 65 will help you complete this quiz. Fill in the best answer in each space provided.

1. When Russia controlled the smallest amount of land, that land surrounded the city

    of _____.

2. Russia expanded into land beyond Moscow to include Novgorod by the end of the

    reign of Czar _____.

3. Kiev became part of Russia by the end of the reign of _____.

4. Russia extended to the Pacific Ocean by the year _____.

5. Lake _____ became part of Russia during

    the reign of Catherine the Great.

6. The Russian seaport of _____ is located on the Sea of Japan.

7. St. Petersburg is located on which major body of water?

    _____

8. This body of water lies north of Russia.

    _____

9. Which sea is surrounded by Russian territory? _____

10. The largest amount of territory was added before the end of the reign of

    _____.

Puzzle Quiz

Each of the questions below is followed by the correct answer. The only problem is that some of the letters have been left out. Fill each blank with a letter to complete the answer. It shouldn't be hard, but you may want to look back over the last few pages to check your spelling.

1. Which German state was the most warlike?

   P __ __ s __ __ a

2. What early traveler to China wrote a famous book about his travels?

   M __ __ __ o   P __ __ __

3. Which hardy sailors reached North America about 500 years before Columbus did?

   V __ __ __ __ g __

4. What is a ruler who has total power called?

   d __ __ p __ __

5. What phrase means that God gave a king the right to rule?

   d __ __ __ n __   r __ __ __ t

6. What was a Russian ruler called?

   c __ __ __

7. What great Spanish fleet did Sir Francis Drake of England help defeat?

   A __ __ __ __ a

8. What Spaniard destroyed the Inca civilization?

   F __ __ __ __ __ s __ __   P __ __ __ r __ __

9. What great sailor sailed around the world and proved it was round?

   F __ __ __ i __ __ __ __   M __ __ __ l __ __ __

10. What is a war called when the opponents are from the same nation?

    c __ __ __ __   w __ __

We've seen how wars were fought over religion and power. Wars were also fought for more land and because of colonies. Spain, England, and France had land in the New World. If these nations were fighting in Europe, they would most likely fight in the New World as well. This was especially true of England and France.

Both England and France wanted new lands for colonies. People living in English colonies in the New World depended on England for supplies. The same was true of France and her colonies. The more colonies a country had, the more goods it could sell to them. Because of the desire for colonies, England and France fought each other off and on for nearly 100 years. France's power in the New World finally ended in 1763, when England got control of Canada.

Revolutions!

When the shooting stopped in 1763, England seemed to have things going its way. It had taken land in the New World from France. The thirteen colonies in the New World were good trading partners. The land in its colonies gave plenty of room for English people to settle.

The people in the English colonies were allowed more freedom than the people in any other nation's colonies. The colonies made most of their own laws. The people who governed them were elected by the voters in the colonies. People of all religions were able to find a place in the colonies where they could live and worship in peace. Things looked good for both England and its colonies.

There were one or two problems, though. Some of the colonists wanted to trade with other countries. England wouldn't allow this. Another problem was that the war with France had cost England a lot of money.

The English king, *George III*, and Parliament decided the colonies should help pay for the war. So they told the colonists that taxes would have to be paid on certain items.

Suddenly, things weren't going well at all between England and its colonies. The colonists said that the tax was not legal, since they could not be in Parliament to vote on taxes. When English tax collectors tried to collect taxes in the colonies, they got chased out of town. Some were covered with tar and feathers. A shipload of tea was dumped into Boston Harbor by angry colonists who weren't willing to pay the tax on tea.

England sent troops to the New World to find the colonists who dumped the tea in Boston Harbor. Then, in April 1775, English soldiers were sent looking for hidden weapons and colonial leaders. The colonists met the soldiers with loaded guns. The *American Revolution* began when American colonists and British soldiers fired upon each other.

On July 4, 1776, the American colonial leaders approved the *Declaration of Independence*. This paper said the colonists were through taking orders from England. They claimed to be a free nation, separate from England.

Boston tea party

But saying something and making it happen were two different things. Colonial troops led by General George Washington fought long and hard. Many people in the colonies and in England felt the war was bad. Both sides lost many men in the fighting.

At times, such as during the terrible winter the American army spent at Valley Forge, things looked hopeless for the new nation. Even with France, Spain, and the Netherlands helping the colonists, it looked as though England might win after all.

It wasn't until 1783 that peace finally came. Then the United States of America was recognized as a new nation.

In 1789, the great *French Revolution* began. The French king, along with a few noblemen and members of the church, ruled the country. Most of the people felt taxes were too high and there was too little chance for working people to live a good life. The people of France saw that the American colonists had been successful in their revolution. They, too, decided to revolt against their king.

The French Revolution lasted until 1799. The fighting between the nobles and the poor people was worse at some times than at others. After the king was killed, the new government tried to get things under control, but it wasn't successful.

When the revolution finally ended, several good things had come about. The French people gained many rights that the English had enjoyed for years. Many of the *peasants*, or poor farmers, finally had land of their own. For the poor people the revolution had been worthwhile.

With the success of the American and French Revolutions as examples, it wasn't long until Spain's colonies also started revolu-

tions. Spanish rule had been harsh and sometimes cruel. People in Spain's colonies in the New World had little freedom. It wasn't surprising that they, too, decided to revolt.

The early 1800's were a time of battle after battle in South America. Such men as *Simón Bolívar* and *José de San Martín* led colonial troops in South America to victory over the armies of Spain. New nations were formed. South America became a continent of *independent* nations. In 1821, Mexico also revolted against Spain and won its independence. Even Portugal lost control of Brazil. The New World had become a world of new nations within a few short years.

Simón Bolívar

Think About It:

The people of North and South America fought in revolutions. So did the people of France. What problems would people face after they overthrew their rulers?

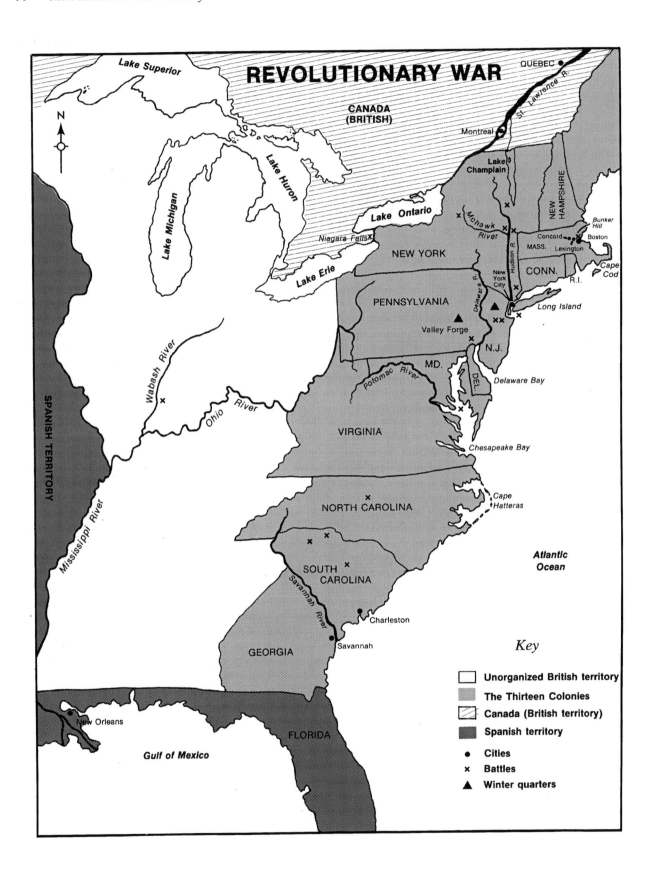

American Revolutionary War Puzzle Quiz

Using the map on page 70 and what you've learned about the American Revolution in this chapter, answer the questions below. Place the answers in the correct places in the puzzle below.

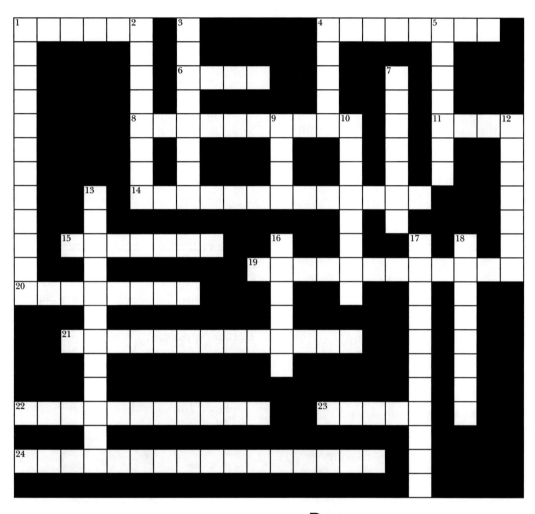

Across

1. Name the country north of the American colonies.
4. Name the river that forms a border between the colonies of South Carolina and Georgia.
6. The large island off the coast of New York and Connecticut is _____ island.
8. Name the city at the mouth of the Mississippi River (2 words).
11. This long river joins the Mississippi River.

Down

1. North Carolina has a necklace of land that sticks out into the Atlantic Ocean. Name that necklace (2 words).
2. Name the body of water to the east of the 13 American colonies.
3. This river forms the border between the colonies of New Jersey and Pennsylvania.
4. This country controlled Florida after the American Revolution.

(continued on page 72)

Across *(continued)*

14. The Potomac River flows into this body of water (2 words).

15. Massachusetts has a finger of land that sticks out into the Atlantic Ocean. Name that finger of land (2 words).

19. The Mississippi River empties into this body of water (3 words).

20. This city is found at the mouth of the Savannah River.

21. The battles of Lexington and Concord took place in this colony.

22. This was the winter quarters in Pennsylvania for the American troops under General Washington (2 words).

23. The smallest of the 13 colonies and still the smallest state is _____ Island.

24. This formed the boundary of Spain's territory in North America in 1783 (2 words).

Down *(continued)*

5. The Hudson River flows through this colony (2 words).

7. This river separates the colonies of Maryland and Virginia.

9. The colony of Pennsylvania touches this Great Lake.

10. This is the westernmost Great Lake.

12. This is the easternmost Great Lake.

13. This famous waterfall lies on the border between New York and Canada (2 words).

16. There are two cities shown on the St. Lawrence River. Name the easternmost city.

17. This body of water separates Delaware and New Jersey (2 words).

18. The Potomac River and the Ohio River form the northern and western borders of this state.

The Beginnings of the Modern World

What happened after the revolutions? New governments were set up and presidents and leaders were chosen. *Constitutions* were written that provided the nations with a set of rules to follow. Things should have settled down, but they didn't.

In 1812, the new United States fought another war with England. The *War of 1812* lasted only a couple of years. Although it really wasn't necessary, it did show the world that the United States was here to stay as a nation!

Great events were taking place in France as well. *Napoleon Bonaparte* had become ruler of France. He made laws and got the country on its feet again after the French Revolution. The people made him *emperor* of France. Then Bonaparte set out to win more land for France. He fought and defeated such nations as Spain and Switzerland. Many of the

German states were conquered by his armies. Then he made a great mistake—he invaded Russia. The terrible Russian winter helped defeat Napoleon's army. The French army was forced to retreat. Napoleon's final end came a few years after his retreat from Russia when the English and German armies defeated him and his men at *Waterloo*.

Napoleon Bonaparte

After Napoleon's defeat at Waterloo, leaders of many European nations met in Vienna. The *Congress of Vienna* attempted to straighten out the problems in Europe. Land taken in war by France was given back to the original owners. Old rulers were given back their countries to rule.

Austria, Italy, and many German states still had problems, though. People wanted more rights and greater freedoms. Sometimes revolutions gave them these rights. Often they didn't.

While things stayed unsettled in Europe, the United States was getting its new government working. After the Revolutionary War ended, George Washington was elected the first president of the United States. White males in the new nation had more rights and freedoms than those in most of the world's other nations.

In spite of these freedoms, troubles developed within the nation. Part of the country kept slaves. For economic as well as humane reasons, other sections of the country thought slavery wasn't a good idea. The two parts of the nation became so angry with each other that in 1861 the United States had its own *Civil War.* This terrible war lasted four years and cost hundreds of thousands of lives. It was one of the worst times in the history of the new country. More Americans died in the Civil War than in World War I and World War II put together! When the Civil War finally ended, the difficult task of rebuilding the country remained. Added to this was the problem of the freed slaves. Many of these people couldn't read or write. Although conditions have improved, some of the social problems that exist today in the United States have their roots in the evils of slavery.

Think About It:

More Americans died fighting the Civil War than died in World Wars I and II. In the World Wars, modern weapons were used. Why did so many Americans die fighting the Civil War?

At about the time the United States was fighting its Civil War, the German states were beginning to join together as a new nation. At times there had been as many as 300 different German states! Each state had its own ruler and its own laws. Except for Prussia, none of these states was very strong.

After years of trying to become strong, these states began to unite. The great Prussian leader *Otto von Bismarck* led Prussia to victory in a war against Austria. After this victory, other German states decided to join Prussia. Within a few years, the new nation of *Germany* was formed. In 1870, this new nation showed its strength by defeating France in a short but bloody war.

At just about the same time, a change was also taking place on a boot of land sticking into the Mediterranean Sea. Here, too, a number of small states were forming a new nation. This nation was called *Italy.*

Austria did not follow the example set by Germany and Italy. Instead of forming a new nation by combining states, Austria divided into two parts and became *Austria-Hungary.*

During all this time, however, a new kind of revolution was beginning. This new revolution has affected your life and mine.

Civil War battle

Review Exercise

Each of the following groups of names or terms has one name or term that does not belong. Find this one item in each group. Underline it.

1. Royal families—Hapsburg, Bourbon, Tudor, Pizarro.
2. New World explorers — Vikings, Marco Polo, Hernando Cortés, Francisco Pizarro.
3. Great leaders of Europe — Louis XIV, Frederick the Great, Simon Bolivar, Napoleon Bonaparte.
4. Leaders of revolutions—George Washington, Jose de San Martin, Simón Bolívar, Hernando Cortés.
5. Great sailors—Vasco da Gama, Ferdinand Magellan, Christopher Columbus, Otto von Bismarck.
6. Words related to France—Napoleon Bonaparte, George III, Waterloo.
7. Words related to the United States—George Washington, War of 1812, Congress of Vienna.
8. Leaders of Russia—Catherine the Great, Peter the Great, Frederick the Great
9. Poor working people—slaves, czars, peasants, serfs.
10. Leaders—despots, emperors, presidents, armadas, czars.

THE INDUSTRIAL REVOLUTION

7

Introduction

"Revolution" means change. "Industry" refers to business, manufacturing, or trade activity. The *Industrial Revolution* brought change to the lives of many people. It didn't involve war, as did the American Revolution. It didn't happen in a few days or even in a few years. It began around 1750 in *Great Britain*. From there it spread to other nations of the world. Its ideas changed the history of the world. Even today, effects of the Industrial Revolution are still changing the way we live.

Machines and Factories

New *machines* led to the Industrial Revolution. They replaced *hand labor* and helped workers *produce* more things faster. Moving water *power* in rivers replaced workers' muscles. One water wheel could turn hundreds of machines.

Machines also started the *factory system*. The new machines were too large and costly to be put in a person's home. Large buildings called *factories* were built to hold many of the machines. The workers in one factory *manufactured* more in a day than one person working in his or her own home could manufacture in a lifetime.

Steam engines began to appear in the 1700's. This important *invention* used wood or coal as *fuel* to heat water in a boiler. Steam from the hot water powered the engine,

which ran the machines. Since a steam engine could be placed anywhere, factories no longer had to be built along rivers. They could be built near fuel, *raw materials*, or *labor*.

Steam engine

As factories produced more, better *transportation* was needed. More *canals* were dug and better roads were built. Here again the steam engine was able to help. By 1830, steam *locomotives* began to pull trains. A few years later, *steamships* carried goods across the sea. The age of rapid transportation was beginning!

Steamship

Think About It:
Why was better transportation needed soon after the factory system started?

75

Great Britain and the Growing Industrial Revolution

There are several reasons why the Industrial Revolution began in Great Britain. There was a large *labor force* of people willing to work in factories. Great amounts of *iron ore* and *coal* were available in Great Britain. Iron ore provided iron and steel, and coal was fuel for steam engines. Rivers helped form *transportation networks* to ship materials. Great Britain also had rich people with money to *invest* in factories.

Great Britain was a *trading* nation that needed many products to sell and trade. The nation's *colonies* were good *markets* for British *goods*.

As years went by, the Industrial Revolution spread to other countries in Western Europe.

It crossed the Atlantic Ocean to the United States.

The revolution itself changed as years passed. Gas-fired engines were more efficient than the steam engines they replaced. Electricity brightened people's lives in many ways. Cars, trucks, and finally the airplane improved transportation. Telegraph, telephone, radio, and television all helped speed *communication.*

Automatic machines made yet another change in industry. And just as coal replaced water power, coal has been replaced in many areas by oil, electricity, and atomic power.

Think About It:

The factory system helped produce more goods. Why did this cause industrial nations like Great Britain to want control over other countries?

Industrial Britain

Use the map of Great Britain on page 79 to answer these questions that factory and ship owners might have asked themselves. Underline the best choice from the three cities given for each question.

1. Which city is a good port?

   Leeds   Bristol   Sheffield

2. Which would probably be the best location for iron and steel mills?

   London   Liverpool   Manchester

3. Iron ore and coal from Wales could be most easily shipped to which city?

   Edinburgh   Bristol   London

4. Which city would likely be the best port for shipping cloth to the United States?

   Liverpool   Newcastle   Leeds

5. In which city would more factories probably be found?

   Newcastle   Edinburgh   Glasgow

6. Which city would be a poor location for iron and steel mills?

   Leeds   Sheffield   London

7. Which location is near both iron ore and coal mines?

   Birmingham   Glasgow   London

8. Which coal mining area does not have iron ore nearby?

   Newcastle   Leeds   Glasgow

9. From which city would ships sail loaded with coal?

   Birmingham   London   Newcastle

10. Ships must sail upriver to reach which port?

   Liverpool   London   Newcastle

Using what you have just read, answer the following questions.

- The following items are important to the Industrial Revolution. Put them in the order in which they appeared.

  steam engine   factory system
  new machines   steam locomotive

- What two raw materials did Great Britain have that helped start the Industrial Revolution?

  _____ and _____.

- Write three or four sentences about the Industrial Revolution, using five or more of these words:

  Great Britain   manufacture   produce
  factory system   power   transportation
  steam engine   market   machines

Money and Wealth

Wealthy people began putting their money together to build bigger factories. The money is called *capital*, and the people who use it are known as *capitalists*. This method of doing things is called *capitalism.*

By the late 1800's, a new way of raising capital began. *Corporations* were formed in which many people invested their money. Bigger factories were built by these corporations. The bigger factories made large profits. The corporations also used their capital (money) to buy smaller factories. Capitalists asked the government for more freedom in running their businesses so they could make greater *profits.*

Before the Industrial Revolution, the government had regulated business. Regulated trade was called *mercantilism.* As the Industrial Revolution grew, however, business owners demanded *less* government control. Such a system is often called *laissez-faire*, a French term that means to let people do as they wish.

Think About It:
Some people wanted government regulation of trade. Others believed in freedom of trade or *laissez-faire*. Why did some people object to freedom in trade?

Businesspeople also believed in *freedom of contract*. This meant that each worker was to meet separately with the employer to discuss wages. The early Industrial Revolution was hard on the workers, but it helped the employers grow rich.

The Industrial Revolution Brings Positive Results

Gradually, some of the bad conditions produced by the Industrial Revolution were changed. First, *labor unions* were formed. They demanded fair wages and decent working conditions for their members. Second, the government in most countries stepped in to make sure factory owners treated their workers well.

One way some governments have made business help workers is through *social security*. This pension system started in European countries and was introduced in the United States in 1935. It provides a certain sum of money each month to retired workers over age 65 (sometimes over age 62). It is gener-

ally based on how much the workers have been earning and how long they've worked. There are pensions also for widows and for others living on the incomes of retired workers. If a wage earner dies before the age of 65, the family receives a pension allowance. A disabled person under 65 can also collect this social security.

A second way federal governments have helped relieve problems stemming from the Industrial Revolution is through *unemployment insurance*. All but the smallest companies are taxed on the wages they pay. When workers become unemployed through no fault of their own, they can collect from the fund for a number of weeks while they are trying to find other work.

There are state laws in the United States that have helped, too. One of these is called *workers' compensation*. These laws make all but the smallest companies insure their workers. This means that they will pay doctor expenses and some wages if the workers are hurt on the job. They also pay money to the families if the workers are seriously hurt or even killed on the job. There are additional state laws that send *inspectors* to work sites to see that factories are as safe and clean as possible.

In these, and in many other ways, governments have helped make the Industrial Revolution valuable to everybody.

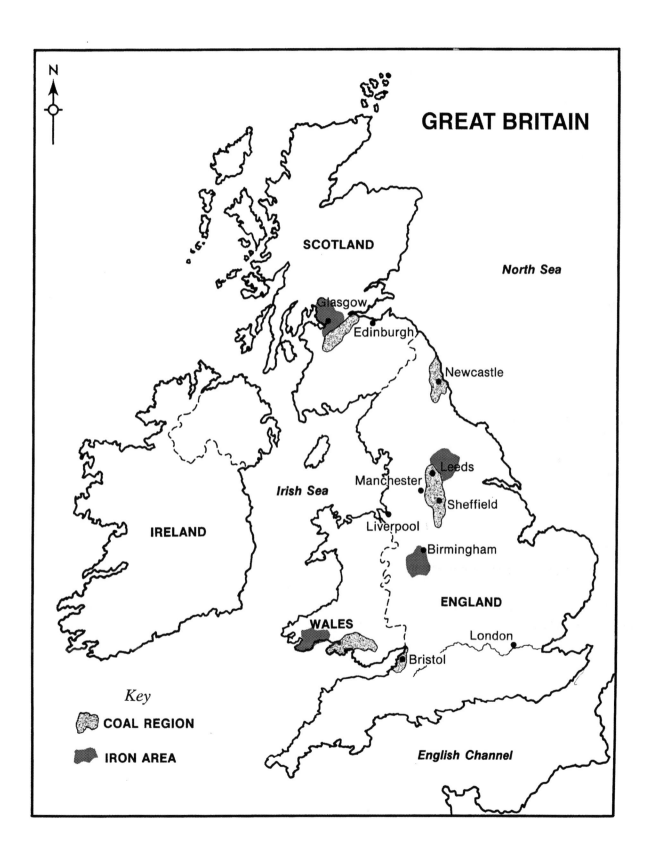

GREAT BRITAIN

SCOTLAND

North Sea

Glasgow

Edinburgh

Newcastle

Leeds

Manchester

Sheffield

Irish Sea

Liverpool

IRELAND

Birmingham

ENGLAND

London

WALES

Bristol

Key

COAL REGION

IRON AREA

English Channel

Puzzle Quiz

Use the words below to answer the puzzle clues that follow. Place the answers in the correct row or column to complete the puzzle on page 81.

canals
capital
capitalism
corporation
factory system
fuel
Great Britain

hand labor
Industrial Revolution
inventions
invested
labor
locomotives
machines

manufacture
markets
power
produce
raw materials
steam engine
transportation

Across

1. A change that affected the way people earned a living (2 words).
4. The Industrial Revolution started here (2 words).
6. Coal and iron ore are _____ _____ (2 words) needed for making things.
7. Getting goods from one place to another requires a _____ system.
8. Manmade rivers used to get goods from the factory to the people.
11. This was needed to make machines run.
12. This replaced the water wheel as power for the new machines (2 words).
13. Steam _____ began to move trains in the 1830's.
14. When you've used your money to help build a factory, you've _____ your money.
15. Money used to build factories.
16. Wood or coal used to power the new machines.
17. When people went to work in a factory, it was called the _____ _____ (2 words).
18. To make or produce goods.

Down

1. The steam engine and other new machines are examples of these.
2. Workers in factories were called this.
3. When work is done by hand, it's called _____ _____ (2 words).
5. Factories were built when these became big and expensive.
8. When a group of people put money together to buy a factory, they formed a _____.
9. The system where money is used by businesspeople to make more money is called _____.
10. Places where goods are sold.
11. To make things is to _____ things.

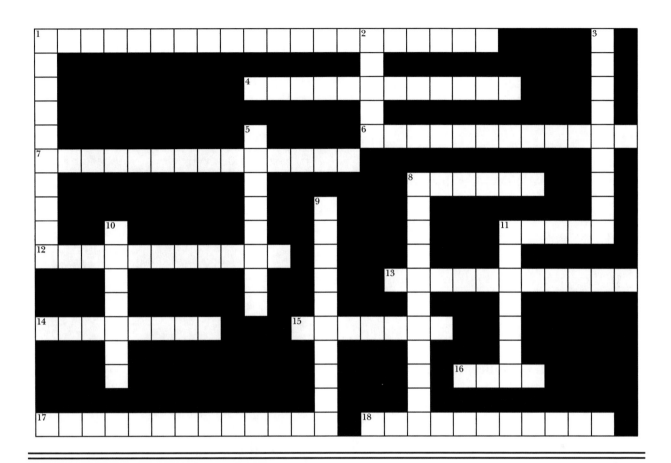

Population Changes

The Industrial Revolution resulted in better farm machines. More food was produced, making it possible to feed more people. This resulted in *population* changes. The better farm machines meant fewer farmers were needed. The farm workers who lost their jobs moved to the cities. Since the factories needed more and more workers, many farmers became factory workers.

During this time medicine also improved. Doctors were better able to care for people. Fewer babies died at birth, and people lived longer. With farmers moving to the cities and people living longer, cities grew rapidly. As factories grew larger, so did cities.

City living was hard on most workers. People were coming to the cities faster than *housing* could be built. Workers and their families often lived in cold, crowded houses. People who slept four in a bed were the lucky ones. The unlucky ones had no bed at all! *Living conditions* were seldom good.

> **Think About It:**
> Why would farmers leave the farm to live in a crowded city?

Working Conditions and Labor Unions

Workers before the Industrial Revolution often worked in their homes. This was called the *domestic system*. Often a person worked part-time. Under the factory system, this wasn't possible. Workers worked all day at a factory. They were paid *wages* by the factory owner in return for their work.

Working conditions were often far worse. Factories were crowded, dirty, and poorly lighted. In the winter, they were usually cold. The money the owners saved on heating resulted in greater *profits.* In addition, people worked 12 to 14 hours a day, 6 or 7 days a week.

Many women and children worked in factories. They were paid less than men for doing the same jobs. Orphans were hired as factory workers, too. Two meals a day and a dirty place to sleep were considered pay enough for them!

In the early 1800's, children as young as six years old could be found working in factories. All too often they didn't have even a lunch hour for resting. They stood at a machine as long as 14 hours. Many were injured or killed when they became tired and fell into moving machinery.

Think About It:

If you were a factory owner, what were some of the ways you could make more money if you didn't care about your workers? What would you do, on the other hand, if you were a *good* factory owner?

Workers knew such things were wrong. They began to form groups called ***labor unions*** to protect themselves. The unions wanted better working conditions and higher wages.

When unions first tried to make changes, laws were passed to stop them. By the late 1800's, these laws were changed. Labor unions grew and became stronger. They helped bring about improved working conditions and better wages for workers.

Think About It:

What would your life be like if you were a factory worker? Why would you become a member of a labor union? Why would you *not* become a member of a labor union?

Florence Nightingale

The Industrial Revolution was not only a time of change in industry. Changes in medicine and care of the sick also took place.

Though she was born in Italy, Florence Nightingale grew up in England. Her father taught her because he wanted her to have a better education than the schools provided.

In 1842, Florence decided to help the needy by working in a hospital as a nurse. Her family objected because nurses came from only the lowest classes in society. They sent Nightingale on a trip in hopes she would forget her desire to become a nurse.

Everywhere Nightingale went, she visited hospitals. When she returned to England she had ideas for improving the terrible hospitals there. Her family finally gave in. Nightingale became superintendent of a private hospital. Among the changes she made was to have hot water available on every floor. She insisted beds be changed so patients could have clean sheets.

England and France declared war on Russia. During this Crimean War, soldiers died of cholera and had operations without anesthesia. Nightingale organized a group of nurses and went to Scutari, Turkey. There she was made head of the nursing staff in the English hospital for wounded soldiers.

Conditions were terrible. Four miles of beds were in the army barracks. Broken bones had not been set. Rats ran over the patients. Medical supplies didn't arrive for six months. Some came after the war ended.

Soon doctors realized if they wanted something done, they had only to ask Miss Nightingale. Soldiers' wives helped by doing the hospital laundry. Nightingale wrote to rich friends in England for money. When she made her night rounds, she carried a lantern.

Within six months the death rate at the hospital dropped from 42 percent to 22 percent. Nightingale opened a library and got paper so the injured could write home.

Because of her work Nightingale became known as the "Angel of the Crimea." She met Queen Victoria and talked about nursing with the monarch. She wrote papers on ways to improve hospitals. Eventually, she opened the Nightingale School and Home for Training Nurses. Graduates of the school went to help other hospitals set up training schools. Over a thousand nurses' training schools were set up in the United States as a result of Nightingale's work and ideas.

The first time the Order of Merit was given to a woman in England, it went to Florence Nightingale. She proved that life could be made better.

Socialism and Communism

Many people thought workers in the 1800's didn't get fair treatment. They thought workers as well as owners should benefit from capitalism.

Some believed that the government should own big businesses. Then everyone would get an equal share in the company's profits. This kind of system is called *socialism.* Under socialism, a government controls certain businesses and regulates prices and wages. The people control the government through the *political party.* They try to elect individuals to government who have the same outlook as they do.

Not all people believed workers could get a share in business by peaceful means. They felt socialism was too slow. Instead of waiting for change by peaceful means, they decided a violent revolution was needed. They wanted to take governments by force. *Karl Marx* from Germany led these people. They were called *Communists.*

Karl Marx wanted workers to have a bigger share of what they produced. He thought capitalism was harmful to workers. His ideas called for workers to take over the government and then give everyone enough to live on.

In 1917, Marx's ideas led to a revolution in Russia. Thousands of people died in that revolution. After the revolution was over, the people found Marx's ideas didn't work the way Marx had hoped. Most people wouldn't exert themselves unless they were paid according to what they did. The very poor were much better off after this revolution, but most workers still weren't as well off as workers in other nations.

Think About It:

Can you think of several reasons why workers would have listened to Karl Marx a hundred years ago? What were the reasons many labor union members didn't follow Marx?

Puzzle Quiz

Use the words below to match the numbered clues. Place the correct words in the right column. Each word should match up with the spaces and the letter provided.

capital	fuel	*laissez-faire*	river
capitalism	housing	locomotive	socialism
communism	inventions	market	steam engine
corporation	invest	mercantilism	trade
employer	labor force	produce	union

1. money   _ _ _ I _ _ _ _

2. put money into   _ N _ _ _ _ _

3. make   _ _ _ D _ _ _ _

4. living quarters   _ _ U _ _ _ _

5. system of government-controlled businesses   S _ _ _ _ _ _ _ _

6. buying and selling goods   T _ _ _ _ _

7. regulated trade   _ _ R _ _ _ _ _ _ _ _ _

8. new discoveries   I _ _ _ _ _ _ _ _ _

9. American economic system   _ A _ _ _ _ _ _ _ _

10. land transportation machine   L _ _ _ _ _ _ _ _ _

11. demand for goods   _ _ R _ _ _ _

12. person who hires workers   E _ _ _ _ _ _ _ _

13. early power source   _ _ V _ _ _

14. investment group   _ O _ _ _ _ _ _ _ _ _

15. workers   L _ _ _ _   _ _ _ _ _

16. coal   _ U _ _

17. human-made power source   _ T _ _ _   _ _ _ _ _ _

18. without restriction   _ _ I _ _ _ _   _ _ _ _ _

19. Karl Marx's system   _ O _ _ _ _ _ _ _

20. organized workers   _ N _ _ _

Puzzle Quiz

Use the words below to answer the questions here and on the next page. When you are through, collect the letters with an **x** under them. Put al! these letters in the blanks at the end of this puzzle on page 87. They spell two words that are the subject of this puzzle.

cities
communication
communism
domestic system
employer
factories
freedom of contract

industry
Karl Marx
labor unions
laissez-faire
living conditions
mercantilism
population

profits
revolution
socialism
transportation
wages
working conditions

1. The movement of goods from the factory to the buyers.

   _ _ _ _ _ _ _ _ _ _ x̲ _ _

2. The exchange of ideas.

   _ _ _ _ _ x̲ _ _ _ _ _ _

3. When people worked at home instead of in factories.

   x̲ _ _ _ _ _ _   _ _ _ _ _ _

4. Because of better farming methods and better medicine, this increased.

   _ _ _ x̲ _ _ _ _ _

5. In this system, the people vote for govern- ment officials who con- trol certain industries.

   x̲ _ _ _ _ _ _ _ _

6. Business, trade, or manufacturing activity.

   _ _ _ _ _ x̲ _ _

7. The money an owner has after paying workers and bills.

   _ _ x̲ _ _ _ _

8. Workers formed these to get better wages and working conditions.

   _ _ _ _   _ _ x̲ _ _ _

9. Pay for a worker.

   _ x̲ _ _ _

10. When government allows businesspeople to run their companies as they wish.

___ __ __ __ __ __ - __ __ __ __ __
   x

11. This man's ideas formed the basis of communism.

__ __ __ __   __ __ __ __
        x

12. The person for whom you work.

__ __ __ __ __ __ __ __
x

13. A big change in conditions or government.

__ __ __ __ __ __ __ __
        x

14. Factories were known for their bad ___ ___.

__ __ __ __ __   __ __ __ __ __ __ __
     x

15. Factory workers moved to the cities, where they had poor ___ ___.

__ __ __ __ __   __ __ __ __ __ __ __
x

16. In this system, workers take over government and businesses after a violent revolution.

__ __ __ __ __ __ __ __
            x

17. Farmers moved here to get factory jobs.

__ __ __ __ __ __
     x

18. A system of regulated trade.

__ __ __ __ __ __ __ __ __ __
                x

19. More people worked here than on farms.

__ __ __ __ __ __ __
         x

20. In this system, each worker meets separately with his or her employer to discuss wages.

__ __ __ __ __ __   __ __   __ __ __ __ __ __ __
                        x

__ __ __ __ __ __ __ __   __ __ __ __ __ __ __ __

THE BEGINNING OF MODERN WORLD PROBLEMS

Introduction

The late 1800's and the early 1900's were a time of world change. Powerful European countries were taking colonies on other continents. China and Japan were again entering world affairs. Several nations feared neighboring nations. The countries of the world began to line up against each other. In 1914, much of the world went to war. Millions of people died in the terrible war and the problems weren't solved. Most of the problems of the world then are still with us today.

Empire Building

As you recall, the United States came to exist because of *empire building*. England, along with France, Spain, and other countries of Europe, wanted new lands and their riches. This desire for colonies didn't stop with the American Revolution. In fact, the Industrial Revolution created a need for colonies that was greater than ever.

Empire building, or adding of colonies, was called *imperialism*. Starting new colonies was expensive and often dangerous. Bloody revolutions, such as the American Revolution, were fought when colonies demanded their freedom. Colonies had to be protected so other nations wouldn't take them over. However, imperialism had some benefits.

Industrial nations manufactured many products that had to be sold. Since colonies didn't generally have factories, they had to buy manufactured goods. Many colonies were forced to buy all their goods from the *mother country*. In this way, imperialism guaranteed a market for goods.

Also, as companies made money from industry, they needed a good place to invest their profits. What better place was there to invest money than in a colony? Rich people in the mother country made money from the things a colony produced. They also made money shipping the raw materials to the mother country. Then they made more money shipping the manufactured products back to the colony.

> **Think About It:**
> Imperialism helped the mother country. Were there ways it helped the colonies as well?

The colonies also provided a place for people to live. Many small European nations had too many people. They were *overpopulated*. A new colony gave people, especially poor people, a place to start a new life. Since they all came from one nation, these people were still interested in the mother country.

Another factor behind imperialism was *national pride*. National pride caused some nations to try to gain too many colonies. It caused hard feelings between nations. It even caused wars.

> **Think About It:**
> After Great Britain lost the United States as a colony, why did it continue to add colonies all over the world?

Victoria

Victoria should never have been queen. When Victoria was born in 1819, she was not in line to become the next ruler of England. Her uncles—George, the Prince Regent; the Duke of York; and the Duke of Clarence—would all rule before she would. If they had children, their children would rule. Thus Victoria was not educated for the throne.

In 1820, Prince George became king when his father died. In 1827, the Duke of York died without children. In 1830 King George IV died and William, the Duke of Clarence, became king. His children were dead. Next in line was Victoria. Her education was changed at once. She was taught the things a queen needed to know. She spoke three languages so she could talk with many foreign people. She was not told she might some day be queen until she was 15. When Victoria was told, she said she would try to be the best queen in history.

King William died when Victoria was 18. She became the ruler of the most powerful nation on earth. Victoria soon became the favorite of the English people. They were happy when she married her cousin, Albert. Customs of the times demanded that the queen propose to Albert. He accepted and they were married. It was a happy marriage. In their life together, they had nine children. These chldren would one day rule many European countries. The descendants of Victoria would control nations fighting one another in World War I.

Although Victoria was loved by her people, she was also the target of assassins. The first time was in 1840. Two shots were fired and both missed. Somehow, the queen always escaped injury when firearms were involved. Later in her life she was attacked by an Irishman who hit her with his cane. He was quickly captured, but not before Victoria got a black eye.

The hardest thing for Victoria to face was life without Albert. He died in December 1861. Victoria thought she might go insane with grief. She ruled England for 39 years after Albert died and always wore black in his memory.

Her most able minister was Disraeli. He advised her and helped her through many a crisis.

Many things happened during Victoria's 63-year reign. The Suez Canal was purchased. India became a British colony. Two wars were fought: the Crimean War with Russia and the Boer War in South Africa. The Industrial Revolution brought many changes in factories and the way things were made.

Victoria died in 1901. She left her children and grandchildren to rule during the First World War. The Victorian Era, a period named for Victoria, also ended. She had became queen when the people neither liked nor respected the throne. During her reign Victoria became the symbol of Great Britain's greatness.

East Meets West

In China, Western economic interests forced changes on an ancient civilization. The Ch'ing Dynasty had confined all foreign trade to one city, Canton. Also, for many years the Chinese had made European nations pay a high tax to trade with them. And China was a huge market. Population had increased to 400 million by 1850.

China was not an industrialized nation. The Ch'ing empress who ruled the country for the last half of the nineteenth century was very conservative. She did not keep up with the changes that the Industrial Revolution had brought to Europe.

The Imperial Palace

England wanted access to this market. When England began producing more goods as a result of the Industrial Revolution, English traders demanded easier rules and lower taxes on trade. What England did next was not very ethical. English traders imported opium, a powerful drug, into China. When the Chinese government tried to stop this, the countries went to war. The English won the war. Treaties with Western powers forced unequal trade burdens on the Chinese. They started owing Western traders more than these traders owed them—for the first time in Chinese history. By the 1890's, foreign nations were carving China up. The English were given Hong Kong, which they kept for over 100 years. The Japanese took the island of Formosa.

In 1900, the Ch'ing Dynasty tried one last time to expel, or throw out, foreigners. However, not only did the Chinese lose the Boxer Rebellion, they were also forced to pay the West several hundred million dollars to cover the damage caused. Very soon after that, the Ch'ing Dynasty collapsed. With it ended a dynastic system that had lasted over 2,000 years.

> **Think About It:**
> Do you think that what happened to the Chinese in the second half of the nineteenth century may have influenced how they feel about Western capitalism even today? Why or why not?

Since before the Industrial Revolution, the British East India Company had controlled all of India's trade. In time, Great Britain took control of India's government, too.

Japan was another story. Until 1854, it traded with no Western nations. In that year, *Matthew Perry* sailed from the United States to Japan with seven warships. Partly because of the ships and partly because of a gift of a model railroad to the ruler of Japan, the Japanese began to trade with the United States. In a few years, several European nations were also trading with Japan.

Japan came to have its own Industrial Revolution. In a few short years, it became a powerful manufacturing nation. In 1894 and 1895, it defeated China in a war over Korea. In 1904 and 1905, it defeated Russia in the Russo-Japanese War.

In 1898, the United States defeated Spain in a short war. From this war the United States took control of the Philippine Islands, Cuba, Puerto Rico, and Guam.

Other nations, too, had empires. France ruled Indochina. The Netherlands ruled the islands of the East Indies. England governed several small nations around India. Which industrial nation of Europe didn't have large land holdings in Asia? The answer is Germany.

Think About It:

What might be some reasons for all the wars we have just read about?

Puzzle Quiz

The answers to the following questions are taken from this chapter. The mixed-up letters that follow the questions, when unscrambled, spell out the correct answers.

1. What is another name for empire building?   ialperismim

2. What name may be used for a nation that owns a colony?   erthmo uncotry

3. What Asian nation did Great Britain defeat in 1842?   nicha

4. What nation did the United States defeat in 1898?   anisp

5. What important nation of Europe felt left out in Asia?   maynreg

6. What was one reason the people of a nation wanted their country to have many colonies?   alnation riped

7. What words describe a country with too many people?   reovlaupopted

8. What city did England take from China in 1842?   nogh onkg

9. Which island nation in Asia became a major industrial country in about fifty years?   aapjn

10. Which huge nation in Asia did England rule for many years?   diian

Europe in Africa

Early European traders went to Africa for things like gold, ivory, and pepper. Soon they began to trade for slaves as well. The Africans used and sold slaves themselves. Now they had a new market.

The *Portuguese* began trading for slaves in West Africa. Millions of slaves were shipped across the Atlantic to the New World. Great Britain and France made slave trading illegal in the early 1800's, but it went on until the 1870's.

The East African slave trade began two thousand years ago. The *Swahilis* were major traders. When the Portuguese took control of Swahili cities, the *Arabs* helped drive the Europeans out. Then the Arabs and Swahilis joined together as slave traders.

The city of *Zanzibar* was the slave trading center. It was not until the 1880's that the British and French were able to force an end to the East African trade in human beings.

Think About It:
Long before Europe and America traded in slaves, Africans and Arabs sold Africans as slaves. Why do we sometimes forget that the slave trade began two thousand years ago?

Many Europeans saw Africa as a new land to explore. Dr. *David Livingstone* was one such person. Beginning in 1841, he traveled and wrote about Africa as he worked as a missionary.

Most Europeans were more interested in trade. To protect their trade, nations began to take control of the lands in which they traded. In the 1870's, Britain, France, Portugal, Germany, and other European nations began to *colonize* Africa. These *empires* were set up to protect trade and give power to the nations of Europe.

In 1884, European nations drew up a plan to divide Africa among them. They divided the continent into colonies but did not pay any attention to the people living there. New colonies divided tribes. Often tribes that hated each other were combined into one colony. In this way Europe did a lot to cause conflict in Africa in future years.

Think About It:
Why did European Nations think they had the right to colonize Africa?

The map on page 101 shows the way in which European countries controlled Africa in 1914. Take a good look at the colonies controlled by Germany. Compare this with the land held by France and Great Britain. Keep this in mind when you read about World War I.

Africa in 1914

The answers to this quiz can be found on the map on page 94.

1. How many European countries held land in Africa in 1914?

   a) 3   b) 5   c) 7   d) 9

2. What body of water is north of the continent of Africa?

   a) Red Sea   b) Indian Ocean   c) Mediterranean Sea   d) Atlantic Ocean

3. Africa is west of this continent:

   a) Europe   b) Asia   c) South America

4. Most of northwestern Africa was controlled by the:

   a) British   b) French   c) Germans   d) Spaniards

5. The Nile River flows through land that was controlled by the:

   a) British   b) French   c) Germans   d) Spaniards

6. Madagascar, which is an island off the coast of Africa, was colonized by the:

   a) British   b) French   c) Spaniards   d) Belgians

7. The people who had the greatest number of colonies in Africa in 1914 were the:

   a) British   b) French   c) Germans   d) Italians

8. The people with the least amount of land colonized in Africa in 1914 were the:

   a) Belgians   b) Spaniards   c) Portuguese   d) Italians

9. The Spanish colonial claims were:

   a) in the north   c) spread over a wide area in Africa

   b) in the south   d) located in the center around the Congo River valley

10. Across the northern part of Africa is the _____ Desert.

11. In 1914, the only two countries in Africa that the Europeans did *not* control were

    _____ and _____ .

12. This river starts in central Africa and flows north into the Mediterranean Sea.

    _____ .

13. What was the name of the river that Belgium controlled? _____

How to Start a War

Before 1850, Germany wasn't a nation. It was a collection of small countries ruled by different people. By the time Germany became *unified* (combined these little countries into one nation), it was too late to build a large empire. But Germany wanted colonies of its own. This desire was one cause of World War I.

We have seen how Great Britain controlled the trade of weaker nations. Whenever two strong nations tried to control the trade of a third nation, there was likely to be trouble. This was the case with Germany and Great Britain. Their struggle for new markets was called *economic rivalry*. This, too, led to World War I.

When national pride went too far, the people of a nation would believe their country was always right. They often came to dislike other countries. Here, then, was another reason for World War I.

Great Britain and Germany both had huge navies. Each tried to become better and more powerful than the other. This was called the *arms race*. These two countries and other nations of Europe had large armies. When nations have strong armies and navies, it's only a matter of time until they find a way to use them.

The troubles on the *Balkan Peninsula* bothered all of Europe. The Ottoman Empire controlled part of that area. Several small nations shared the rest of the peninsula. Just like little children with big brothers, these small nations had big friends, or *allies*. Russia was a big friend to some of them. Austria-Hungary was friendly to others. When the little nations got into fights, their big allies nearly came to blows, too.

Just as people join clubs, so did the nations of Europe. Their "clubs" were called *alliances*. Germany, Austria-Hungary, and Italy joined together in the *Triple Alliance*. Great Britain, France, and Russia formed the *Triple Entente*. Each member of the gang or alliance promised to help the other members in case of trouble.

All that was needed for war to begin was a spark to set things off. That spark came on June 28, 1914. *Francis Ferdinand*, Archduke of

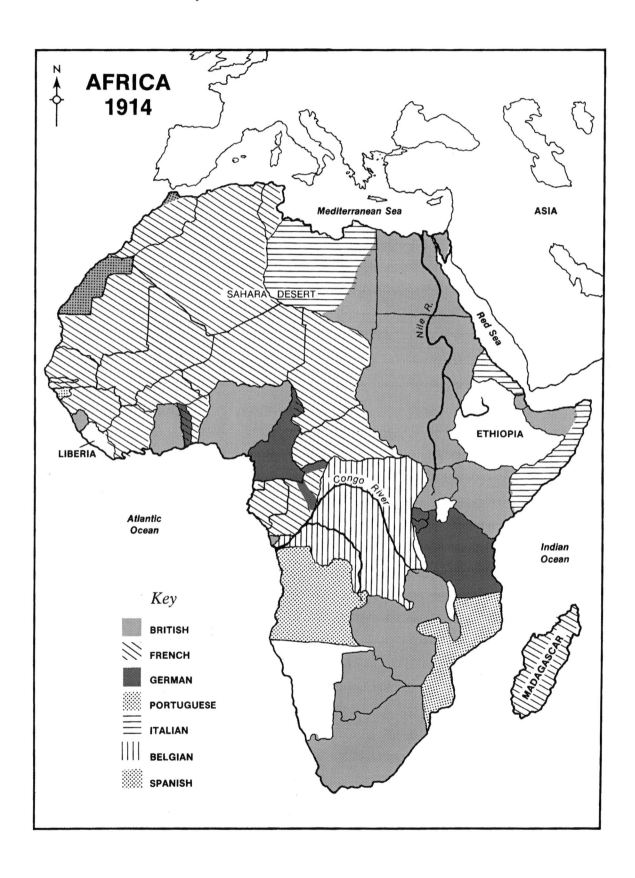

AFRICA 1914

N

Mediterranean Sea

ASIA

SAHARA DESERT

Nile R.

Red Sea

ETHIOPIA

LIBERIA

Atlantic
Ocean

Congo River

Indian
Ocean

MADAGASCAR

Key

BRITISH

FRENCH

GERMAN

PORTUGUESE

ITALIAN

BELGIAN

SPANISH

Austria-Hungary, was visiting the little nation of *Serbia*. A murderer *assassinated* him. One month later Austria declared war on Serbia.

Think About It:

The nations of Europe made several mistakes that helped to cause World War I. List these mistakes. Are the nations of the world making any of the same mistakes today? If so, check the mistakes that are still being made.

The World at War

Francis Ferdinand was killed in the summer of 1914. Austria Hungary used his murder as an excuse to declare war on Serbia. By August 1914, Austria-Hungary and Germany were at war with Great Britain, France, and Russia. Germany and her supporters were now known as the *Central Powers*. The nations fighting them were called the *Allies.*

Germany defeated the little country of Belgium and invaded France. Great Britain rushed to the aid of France. Germany was fighting Russia on the east at the same time it fought France and Great Britain on the west. The western fighting line was called the *Western Front*. Great ditches called *trenches* were dug. The armies put up barbed wire and brought up guns. All Europe prepared for a long, terrible war.

Some nations, such as Switzerland, didn't take sides but stayed *neutral*. Others joined sides. The Ottoman Empire helped Germany. Italy joined the Allies against the Central Powers in an attempt to gain more land. Japan joined the Allies, hoping to gain some of Germany's colonies.

The United States decided to stay neutral. Germany, however, began using its *submarines* to sink ships bringing supplies to the Allies. On May 7, 1915, the ship *Lusitania* was sunk in the Atlantic Ocean by a German submarine. Of the 1,198 passengers who died, 139 were Americans. In March 1917, three American ships were sunk in two days. Two weeks later the United States declared war on Germany.

By June 1917, American troops were arriving in France. France and Great Britain greatly needed their help. After many battles, the Allies and Germany signed an *armistice*, or an agreement to stop fighting. On November 11, 1918, World War I was over. Some 30 nations had been involved in the war. Over 10 million people had died and twice that many had been wounded. No one knows how many people lost their homes and farms in the fighting.

Think About It:

Millions of soldiers died in the trench warfare of World War I. How did modern weapons, such as tanks and bombers, bring an end to trench fighting in later wars?

World War I made several "firsts." It was the first time the nations of the world joined sides to fight against each other. It was the first time that submarines were used in large numbers. It was also the first time that airplanes were used in warfare. They didn't look much like the airplanes of today—they had upper and lower wings and were quite small. Another new invention used in this war was the tank. It looked like an armored car and could go across the tops of the trenches. Poison gas was another invention. It was difficult to use because the wind often shifted and soldiers might end up poisoning themselves.

- Use the following words to help you write a short report on World War I and its causes.

alliance	assassinate
Allies	Central Powers
armistice	economic rivalry
arms race	neutral

Airplane used in World War I

Europe in 1914

Study the map on page 98 carefully. You will have to use the key to answer these questions.

1. Before the start of World War 1, European countries joined "alliances" as protection against other nations. Name the three countries that formed the Triple Entente.

    a) _____ b) _____ c) _____

2. Three other countries joined together to become the Triple Alliance. Name the Triple Alliance nations.

    a) _____ b) _____ c) _____

3. World War I actually started in Serbia, which was one of six nations on the Balkan Peninsula. (A small portion of the Ottoman Empire was on the Peninsula as well.) Locate the Balkan Peninsula, which is outlined, and name the other nations —besides Serbia—on it.

   a) Serbia   c) _____   e) _____

   b) _____   d) _____   f) _____

4. After the war broke out, the members of the Triple Alliance became known as the Central Powers. What is the one nation that belonged to the Triple Alliance but did *not* join the Central Powers? _____

5. Five of the nations located on the Balkan Peninsula joined the members of the old Triple Entente to become the Allied nations. What country on the Balkan Peninsula joined the Central Powers? _____

6. South of the Black Sea was another nation that joined the Central Powers. This country was _____ .

7. Seven nations are shown on the map that belonged to neither the Central Powers nor the Allied nations. What are these nations called? _____

8. This Allied nation isn't connected to the continent of Europe; it's an island off Europe's coast. Name this island country. _____

9. Germany borders two seas that its navy could use in wartime. Name these two seas.

   a) _____   b) _____

10. What Allied nation could stop Germany's navy by blocking the outlets where the North Sea joins the Atlantic Ocean? _____

11. What would be the best reason for Germany, Austria-Hungary, Bulgaria, and the Ottoman Empire to be called the Central Powers?

    a) Many of them were located near the center of Europe.

    b) They were all grouped together in one area with no Allied country separating them.

    c) Some of the small Allied nations were in the center of the Balkan Peninsula.

12. The largest of the Allied Powers was _____ .

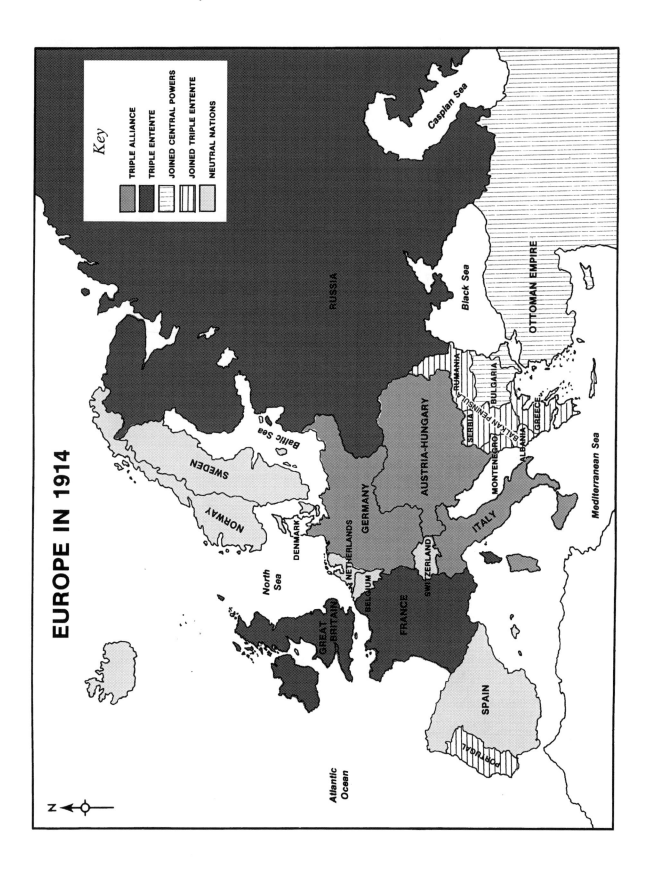

EUROPE IN 1914

The Russian Revolution, Chinese Nationalism, and a Plan for Peace

While World War I was in full swing, events were happening in Russia that changed the course of the world. In November 1917, the Communists led a revolution against the Russian government. The people were promised land, a share in the factories, and peace. Their leader, *V. I. Lenin*, was a follower of Karl Marx.

The revolution brought death to many Russians. It changed the lives of every person in Russia. However, it did bring a kind of peace. In March 1918, the Russians signed a *peace treaty* with Germany.

World attention was on the war in Europe. In China a major change was taking place which many people ignored. Most Chinese resented the Europeans and Japanese. Many began to support the *Nationalists*, who wanted foreign rule to end. By 1912, the Nationalists took control of China's government. There were still small armies controlled by bandit warlords throughout China at this time.

In 1925, *Chiang Kai-shek* took control of the Nationalist party. European governments liked the young general, as did rich Chinese landowners. The new leader fought the warlords and defeated them. He also fought a group called the Communists. These he did not defeat.

During World War I few people had any idea how events in China would later affect the entire world.

When Germany sent all its troops to France, things looked bad for the Allies. United States soldiers helped the Allies to win the war in the fall of 1918.

When the war ended, the problems of keeping peace began. The president of the United States, *Woodrow Wilson*, had some good ideas. He called them his *Fourteen Points*. He wanted all lands to be free from fear of other nations. He wanted freedom to trade and an end to the arms race. People living in colonies were to be helped to set up governments of their own. Most important, a *League of Nations* was to be set up so nations of the world could solve their problems by reason rather than by war.

President Woodrow Wilson

Many of the Allies didn't like President Wilson's ideas. They wanted Germany to be punished for the war and to pay for war damages (reparations). On top of that, the United States refused to join the League of Nations.

When the *Treaty of Versailles* ended the war in the summer of 1919, many of President Wilson's ideas for peace were left out. Germany lost its colonies in Asia and Africa. Some German land was to be used by France. Austria and Hungary became two completely separate nations. Other new nations were formed. The United States didn't even sign the peace treaty.

Think About It:

Germany had to pay for war damages and give up land after the war ended. New nations were formed from parts of other nations. How did these things cause hatreds that helped lead to another war?

had learned little from that terrible war. In another 20 years, nations of the world were again fighting instead of thinking out and discussing their problems.

The war was over, but the world's problems were not. Hate and bitterness still filled the hearts of many. It seemed that the world

Think About It:

Why would countries such as France want to punish Germany at the end of the war? Could they be blamed for feeling angry toward Germany?

Review Exercise

Decide which of the two events happened first in each of the following pairs of events. Look back over the unit if you don't remember. Underline the event that came first.

1. The English fought a war with China.
   Japan defeated Russia in a war.

2. The United States fought Spain.
   Japan fought China.

3. The Triple Entente was formed.
   World War I was fought.

4. Germany became part of the Triple Alliance.
   Germany was one of the Central Powers.

5. Francis Ferdinand was assassinated.
   The European arms race began.

6. Trenches were dug on the Western Front.
   The Communist Revolution took place in Russia.

7. The *Lusitania* was sunk.
   The United States entered the war against the Central Powers.

8. An armistice was signed between the Allies and Germany.
   The Treaty of Versailles was signed.

9. President Wilson presented his Fourteen Points.
   Lenin led the Russian people to revolt against the government.

10. Germany was unified.
    Austria and Hungary became separate nations.

THE WORLD IN THE TWENTIETH CENTURY

Introduction

A long, terrible war had just ended. The people of Russia had just finished a bloody revolution. New nations had been formed. Old nations had new borders. Plans for world peace had been talked about. The world wanted peace, but peace didn't come for any length of time. Why? That was the question people asked themselves.

Russia After the Revolution

In 1917, Lenin became the leader of Russia. He wanted to make Russia work as Marx had said communism should work. The government was to own all land, factories, mines, and stores. However, in a very short time, Lenin could see the plan wasn't working. Less food and fewer goods were produced than before the Russian Revolution.

In order to help the country, Lenin began to let people buy and run some of the businesses. Farmers could sell extra food they grew and keep the profits. Things began to improve almost at once. The ideas of capitalism were being used in a Communist country!

In December 1922, Russia became the *Union of Soviet Socialist Republics*, or the Soviet Union. This meant that all areas of Russia were now ruled by one leader. The Soviet Union was a *dictatorship*. One person ruled the country with the help of a few advisers. Only members of the *Communist party* could say anything about the government.

In 1924, *Joseph Stalin* became leader of the Soviet Union. He started the *Five-Year Plans*. The idea behind these plans was to increase farm and factory production by setting goals for five-year periods. The plans worked very well, and the Soviet Union soon became a powerful industrial nation.

Lenin Square, downtown Tbilisi

Everything wasn't good for the Soviet people, though. Stalin began to place more government controls on his people. He made the Soviet Union into a *police state*. The Communist party controlled the police. If people didn't obey the government, the secret police arrested them. They were then either put in prison, sent to *Siberia* to work for the government, or killed.

The World After the War

Great Britain and France had been on the winning side of World War I. Even so, they were little better off than Germany. The British had used great amounts of money and materials to fight the war. The United States and Japan had more modern factories and were soon taking trade away from Great Britain.

Since much of the war had been fought in France, that nation suffered terrible losses. France rebuilt quickly, however, and soon was doing well. If the French government had been strong, France would have kept on doing well. But the government of France changed every few months, and the country could never become strong.

Think About It:
Great Britain, France, and the United States were winners in World War I. Why didn't the United States suffer economically as much as the other two nations?

Germany had to begin paying for the damage it had caused during the war. French soldiers were sent to the *Ruhr*, a part of Germany where coal mines and steel mills

were located. The German workers went on *strike*. The soldiers went back to France and the workers went back to work.

Many other countries did not recover as quickly as France. Austria and Hungary were both weak. The Balkan nations, such as Yugoslavia, Bulgaria, and Albania, were small and had little industry. Poland came under the control of an army general who dictated the country's policies. Italy's king was weak and the country didn't do well. Spain went from king to dictator to republic to dictator again.

Worst of all, much of the world suffered a great *depression* beginning about 1929 and lasting for several years. People lost jobs. Banks closed and people lost their money. People became discouraged and bitter. The world was ready for a change.

Think About It:
Read the first paragraph of this section again. Tell in your own words why you believe the first two sentences are true or false.

Europe, 1919–1929,
Between World War I and World War II

Great changes occurred in the map of Europe because of the Versailles Treaty, which ended World War I. You'll need to compare the map on page 104 with the map of Europe in 1914 (page 98) to answer the starred questions. Underline the correct answers or, when necessary, write them in the space provided.

1. East of Norway and Sweden a new country was created named:

   a) Poland   b) Rumania   c) Denmark   d) Finland

*2. Finland was created out of territory that belonged to what nation in 1914?

   a) Sweden   b) Germany   c) Russia   d) Austria-Hungary

3. Before the end of World War I, Russia had a revolution and dropped out of the war. After the revolution, the country's name was changed to the

   _____.

4. South of Finland and east of the Baltic Sea, three more new countries were formed. These countries were:

   a) Norway, Sweden, and Denmark   c) Poland, Czechoslovakia, and Hungary
   b) Estonia, Latvia, and Lithuania

*5. These three countries were formed out of territory that belonged to what nation in 1914?

   a) Sweden   b) Germany   c) Russia   d) Austria-Hungary

6. The country of Germany was in two parts, separated by this country:

   a) Poland   b) Czechoslovakia   c) Rumania   d) Denmark

*7. Poland was formed from territory held by two countries in 1914. These nations were:

   a) Austria, Hungary   b) Germany, Russia   c) Turkey, Austria   d) France, Germany

*8. The Austria-Hungarian Empire was divided into four countries. Two were Austria and Hungary. The other two new countries were:

   a) Czechoslovakia, Poland   c) Yugoslavia, Rumania
   b) Czechoslovakia, Yugoslavia   d) Rumania, Bulgaria

*9. Compare Rumania in 1914 and in 1929 and decide what is correct:

   a) Rumania was given land belonging to Turkey.
   b) Rumania was smaller in 1914 than it was in 1929.
   c) Rumania was larger because German land was given to it.

*10. Serbia, Montenegro, and part of Austria-Hungary were put together and called:

   a) Czechoslovakia   b) Albania   c) Rumania   d) Yugoslavia

11. Germany and Austria-Hungary lost a lot of territory at the end of World War I. But what Allied nation lost a lot of territory, too?

   a) France   b) Great Britain   c) Rumania   d) Russia

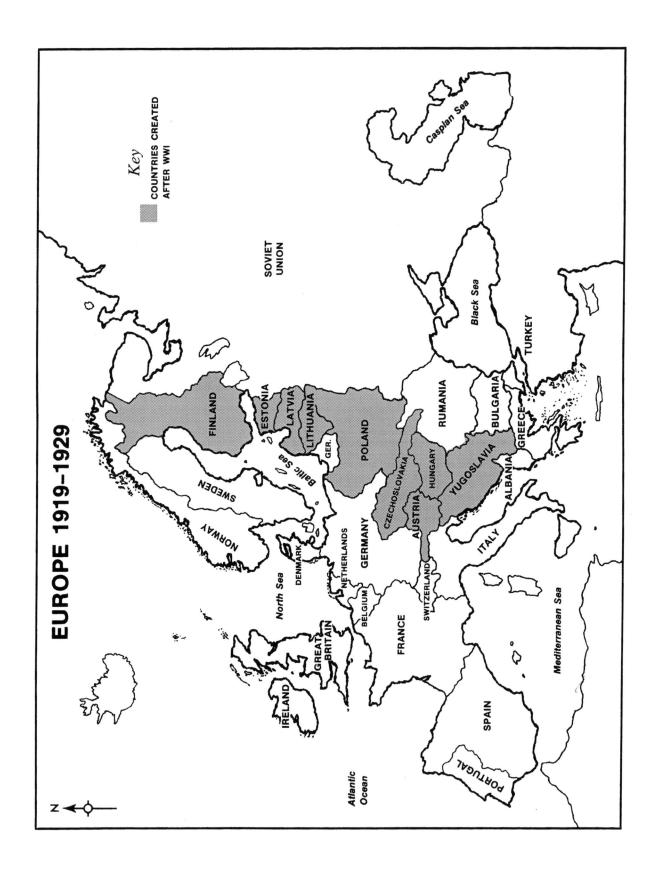

A Time of Change

President ***Franklin D. Roosevelt*** of the United States began the ***New Deal*** to help the United States snap out of the Depression in the 1930's. He got Congress to pass laws helping workers. These laws limited working hours and set fair wages for workers. They also helped labor unions grow stronger.

The government tried to help the farmers, too. Laws were passed to raise the prices for farm crops. Farmers could also get loans from the government to improve their farms.

Homeowners got loans from the government to help buy houses. The government built low-cost housing for people. Out-of-work people were hired by the government to work on ***public works projects***, such as parks and roads. The ***social security*** program made sure older workers would have an income after they were too old to go on working.

Franklin D. Roosevelt with farmers

Slowly, the United States began to gain strength and get over the bad effects of the Depression. But what was happening outside of the United States at this time?

Long before World War I, Great Britain had given such countries as Canada, Australia, and New Zealand numerous rights that allowed them largely to govern themselves.

Soon after the war, these nations got complete freedom. Other nations, such as India, were prepared for self-government. All these countries and the colonies of Great Britain joined the ***Commonwealth of Nations***. They would trade together and help each other as much as possible.

Because of the Depression, Germans became discouraged with their government. It couldn't solve the problems that the Depression brought. A World War I soldier named *Adolf Hitler* started a new political party that promised to solve these problems. It was the *National Socialist party*, which was soon called the *Nazi party*. By 1933, Hitler had taken complete control of Germany and become its dictator. One of the ways he helped end Germany's depression was to build a huge army and navy. This provided jobs for people without work. It also helped the country by creating jobs for people in mines, steel mills, and gun factories. Hitler ended a depression by getting ready for a war!

In Italy a man named *Benito Mussolini* set up the *Fascist party*. By 1922, Mussolini had complete control of the government of Italy. As its dictator, he used the secret police to keep the people in fear of the government.

In 1936, *General Francisco Franco* led a revolution in Spain. A terrible civil war followed. During this time people fought their fellow countrypeople. When it ended in 1939, Franco was dictator of Spain.

> **Think About It:**
> Dictators often gain power during economic depressions. Why are people more willing to accept a dictator during a depression?

> **Think About It:**
> How would putting people in the army give workers in mines, steel mills, and gun factories more work?

Adolf Hitler

Puzzle Quiz

The letter maze below contains 12 words that are important names and terms in this chapter. They may appear vertically or horizontally in the maze. Some of the words cross others. Can you find all 12? Circle them. The following clues tell you what to look for.

1. Russian leader before Stalin

2. Russian leader who started the Five-Year Plans

3. United States president who started the New Deal

4. Short name for the National Socialist party of Germany

5. Name of Italian dictator

6. Spanish dictator after Spain's civil war

7. German dictator

8. Benito Mussolini's political party

9. Part of Russia where prisoners were sent to work for punishment

10. Part of Germany where most coal mines and steel mills were found

11. Name for the nations that belonged to Great Britain or had belonged to Great Britain

12. Name for any person who has complete power over the people of a nation

C	R	M	O	R	B	T
O	O	U	C	A	D	H
M	O	S	N	D	I	N
M	S	S	A	D	C	U
O	E	O	R	S	T	A
N	V	L	F	T	A	I
W	E	I	N	A	T	R
E	L	N	A	L	O	E
A	T	I	Z	I	R	B
L	E	N	I	N	H	I
T	S	T	E	I	U	S
H	I	T	L	E	R	J
F	A	S	C	I	S	T

The End of World Peace

President Wilson's plan for peace had included a League of Nations. Member nations would bring their problems to the League and discuss them. The idea was good, but it didn't work. One of the reasons why it didn't work was that not all nations joined the League. Although Woodrow Wilson thought the League was important, the United States didn't join it. Other nations such as Germany withdrew from the League. Also, the League had no way to force nations to change what they were doing.

The League ended in 1936 when Ethiopia, an African nation, was invaded by Italian troops. The ruler of the African nation asked the League for aid. None was given and Ethiopia was occupied by Italy. The League of Nations had failed to keep peace. The world was again ready for war.

Trouble had been brewing for a long time in Asia as well. China had not been able to unite under one leader. *Chiang Kai-shek*, a general, had combined most of China under his rule. Even so, by the early 1930's he was fighting Communist troops that had taken over part of China.

India wasn't happy with British rule. Indians wanted to rule themselves completely. An Indian leader, *Mohandas "Mahatma" Gandhi*, worked for freedom. He didn't believe in fighting. His followers simply refused to obey British orders. He and many of his people went to jail for their beliefs. His *passive resistance* paid off, though. In 1947, India finally became a free nation and a part of the Commonwealth of Nations. Gandhi proved that fighting wasn't the way to settle a problem.

Mohandas Ghandhi

Japan didn't follow Gandhi's ideas. Japan had become more warlike. In 1931, Japanese armies invaded *Manchuria*, a neighbor of China. In 1937, Japan attacked China.

Europe was on the edge of its second terrible war in 20 years. Germany had *rearmed* and was stronger than any other nation of Europe. In 1936, it proved its strength by moving into the *Rhineland*. Germany needed this area for its raw materials. Also in 1936, Hitler and Mussolini signed an alliance to help each other in time of trouble. They were now called the *Axis* powers.

In 1938, Germany invaded and defeated its former friend, Austria. Czechoslovakia was taken by Germany in March 1939. The next month Italy went into Albania.

Any lessons learned from World War I had been forgotten. Europe was at war! Much of Asia was at war! The rest of the world was soon to join sides and follow into war.

Think About It:

When Italy invaded Ethiopia and Albania, the rest of the world did nothing. When Japan invaded Manchuria and China, the rest of the world did nothing. When Germany took Austria and Czechoslovakia, the rest of the world did nothing. Were the nations of the world right or wrong in not helping the smaller nations? Why?

World War II

In August 1939, Germany and the *Soviet Union* signed an agreement to remain friends. On September 1, 1939, *Hitler's* troops, called *Nazis*, attacked Poland. Polish fighters on horseback met German tanks. The outcome was easy to predict. With the help of the Soviet Union, Germany defeated Poland in less than four weeks.

Two days after Germany attacked Poland, the *Allies*—France and Great Britain—declared war on Germany.

At once the world saw Germany display a new kind of effective, lightning-quick warfare. It was called *blitzkrieg*. Between April and June of 1940, German armies took Denmark, Norway, the Netherlands, Luxembourg, Belgium, and France. In August and September of the same year, German airplanes began a terrible bombing of Great Britain. The *Battle of Britain* had begun. The British were led by Prime Minister *Winston Churchill*. They fought the German air force in the skies and won. Adolf Hitler was forced to give up his plan to invade Great Britain. In June 1941, Hitler ordered his troops to attack his old ally, the Soviet Union.

The United States was not involved in the fighting, but it aided Great Britain with the *Lend-Lease Act*. This act made it possible for the United States to lend ships, war supplies, and airplanes to nations fighting Germany.

In September 1940, *Japan* joined the Axis powers. On December 7, 1941, Japan attacked the United States Navy and Air Force at *Pearl Harbor*, Hawaii. On the same day, they attacked the Philippines. The Japanese attack surprised the American forces, and the Navy was almost totally destroyed. The following day the United States declared war on Japan. Three days later, Germany and Italy declared war on the United States.

Think About It:

World War II began in Europe in September 1939. Japan attacked the United States in December 1941. What are some reasons the United States did not declare war on Germany until after the Japanese attack?

Four years of terrible war followed. There was fighting in the Pacific area against the Japanese. There was fighting in Africa and Europe against the Germans and the Italians. Over 17 million people died in battle. Millions of civilians died from sickness, starvation, and bombing.

Life was dreadful for millions of civilians in many parts of the world. Among those who suffered most were the European Jews. Even before the war began, the Nazis had imprisoned or killed most German Jews. During the war the attackers turned to the Jews of occupied countries. The Nazis killed six million Jews in the campaign of hate now known as the *Holocaust*.

On June 6, 1944, the Allies invaded Europe. The army, led by General *Dwight Eisenhower*, landed on the coast of France and began to push the German army back to Germany. This push took almost a year. The Soviet Union advanced from the east, and the United States and Great Britain advanced from the west. Germany finally surrendered to the Allies on May 8, 1945. Adolf Hitler was dead. The German nation was crushed. Berlin, the capital city, was a huge pile of shattered buildings.

The war in the Pacific area continued. The United States forces were led by General *Douglas MacArthur.* Japan refused to surrender. Hard and difficult fighting was needed to recapture the islands Japan had taken over. This effort was called "Island Hopping." But to end the war, it appeared as though the Allies would have to invade Japan itself. This would result in a great loss of Allied lives because the home islands of Japan had been built up to resist such an invasion. However, on August 6, 1945, President *Harry S. Truman*

of the United States carried out a threat that had been made to Japan. He ordered a new and terrible weapon to be used against the Japanese. On August 6, the first *atomic bomb* was dropped on the Japanese city of *Hiroshima.* The bomb totally destroyed the city and killed tens of thousands of people. Three days later the city of *Nagasaki* was the target of a second atomic bomb. The Japanese knew they could not withstand this new weapon. On August 14, they surrendered. World War II was over.

> **Think About It:**
> President Truman dropped the atomic bomb to save lives. Can you explain this? Maybe it will help to reread the last paragraph above.

Atomic explosion

Puzzle Quiz

Read each of the following puzzle clues. Find the answers in the material you have just read. Write the answers in the correct row or column in the puzzle.

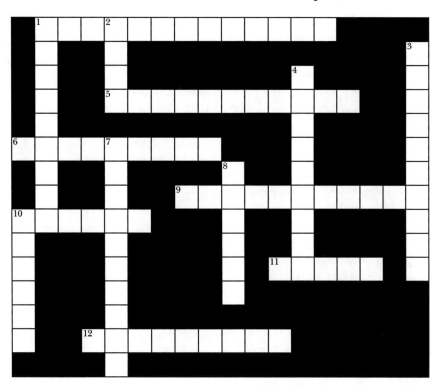

Across

1. Chinese general

5. Hitler invaded the _____ _____ in June 1941.

6. Germany moved into the _____ in 1936.

9. The Japanese attacked _____ _____, Hawaii.

10. France and Great Britain were called this.

11. This nation attacked the United States on December 7, 1941.

12. The _____ _____ Act gave supplies to Great Britain.

Down

1. Winston _____ was prime minister of Great Britain.

2. Germany, Italy, and Japan were the _____ powers.

3. Lightning war

4. The first atomic bomb was dropped on this city.

7. Leader of the Allied invasion on June 6, 1944

8. Mohandas _____ led a nonviolent movement that brought freedom to India.

10. The _____ bomb was a new weapon for World War II.

Winston Churchill (1874–1965)

By the time he was seven, Winston Churchill knew he hated school! Eventually he found a school he did like. That was Sandhurst, which was a military college.

When Winston graduated eighth in a class of 150, he was given an army commission. He served as a soldier and later as a war correspondent.

When the Boer War broke out in South Africa, Churchill was hired by a London newspaper to report the war. Soon after he arrived, the Boers stopped his train and took Churchill prisoner. He broke out of prison and crossed 300 miles of Boer territory to safety.

When Churchill returned to England, he was elected to the House of Commons and his political career began. In 1911, he became First Lord of the Admiralty.

Churchill realized war with Germany was coming. He built up the navy and created a naval air force. When war broke out in 1914, the navy was ready. A year later he urged an attack on the Gallipoli peninsula. It was controlled by Turkey, which had joined Germany in the war.

A successful attack at Gallipoli would have opened the way for English ships to reach Russia. The attack failed. Many lives were lost, and Churchill was in disgrace. He resigned as First Lord of the Admiralty and believed he was a failure.

Between the First and Second World Wars, Churchill remained in politics and became well-known as a painter and writer. Then, in 1939, Germany again plunged the world into war.

On May 10, 1940, King George VI asked Churchill to become prime minister. Churchill was 66 years old. During the summer of 1940, the German air force bombed England day and night. Churchill walked the London streets checking the damage without thought of his own safety.

The British Royal Air Force forced Germany to end its bombing. Churchill knew the war with Germany and Italy would be won. It was his task to give strength to the British people.

After Japan attacked the United States, Churchill met often with President Franklin Roosevelt. They planned not only the war but also how to help the world recover after war ended. Joseph Stalin of the Soviet Union joined in these meetings.

British and U.S. troops were finally ready to invade and free France. Churchill wanted to go on the first boat. Military leaders feared for his life. King George decided to go with Churchill. Churchill told the king he might get killed. The king said Churchill could die. They finally agreed each would remain home because of the danger to the other.

Germany surrendered in May 1945. In the next election the British people voted against Churchill. He was no longer their prime minister.

When the Korean War broke out in 1951, Churchill again became prime minister. He was almost 77 at the time. He resigned in 1955 because of his age.

Queen Elizabeth made Churchill a knight, and the United States made him an honorary citizen. It was the only time in history the U.S. had given this honor.

For a boy who hated school, Churchill achieved great things and will always be remembered as a fighter for freedom.

Another Chance for World Peace

In 1941, President Roosevelt and Prime Minister *Winston Churchill* of England met and agreed to the *Atlantic Charter*. The ideas in this agreement were much like those of the old League of Nations.

In 1945, *delegates* from fifty nations met in San Francisco, California. They added to the ideas found in the Atlantic Charter. When they were finished, the *United Nations* was formed. Its charter went into effect in October 1945. The UN was to be a worldwide peacekeeping organization. It was to have the power to use armed forces to help keep peace.

In addition, the UN would help *underdeveloped* nations with problems of health, farming, and education. By helping poor nations, UN members hoped to make the world a better place for all of us.

With these good ideas, the world looked forward to peace and happiness. During the ten years after the end of the war, some things did go well, but many things went badly.

Japan quickly recovered from the damage done by the war. Its government was changed so one person no longer had complete control over the people. In fact, Japan's government became much like that of the United States. All adults were given the right to vote, and everyone was protected by documents similar to the Bill of Rights.

After the fighting stopped in Europe, Germany was divided. The Soviet Union, France, Great Britain, and the United States each took control of a part of Germany. Soon the United States, France, and Great Britain put their parts of Germany together. This became known as West Germany. The Soviet Union didn't join its part of Germany with the rest. It became known as East Germany.

The western part of Germany changed its government. It became a democracy like the United States. The eastern part of the nation, controlled by the Soviet Union, was Communist.

Communism, as you can see, spread from the Soviet Union. The maps on pages 127 and 135 show which countries became Communist nations.

A new kind of war, the *cold war*, came into being. A cold war doesn't involve huge battles. It is more a battle of words and ideas. For example, on July 24, 1948, the Soviets refused to allow food and supplies to be shipped into the western part of Berlin to care for Allied troops still in Berlin. For over a year, all supplies had to be flown to the western part of Berlin. The *Berlin Airlift* flew 277,264 planeloads of supplies to Berlin during that time. The Soviets finally agreed to allow food and supplies to enter Berlin again. No fighting had occurred, but the United States had won a "battle" in the cold war.

Think About It:

The cold war used words and threats instead of bullets. The United States and the Soviet Union were always ready for war. How could a cold war cost nearly as much to fight as a real war?

A step toward stability came when NATO—the *North Atlantic Treaty Organization*—was formed in 1949. Nations such as Great Britain, France, Canada, and the United States promised to help each other in the event of a Soviet attack. It was hoped this would stop the spread of communism.

In Asia, however, peace never really came. As soon as the war with Japan ended, China had its own civil war. Communists led by *Mao Tse-tung* fought the troops of Chiang Kai-shek. By 1949, the Communists ruled China, which was renamed the *People's Republic of China*. Mao Tse-tung was ruler of the most populated nation in the world. Chiang Kai-shek's government moved to the island of *Formosa* off the coast of China. Formosa soon became known as *Taiwan*.

Mao Tse-tung

Even though unrest troubled much of the world, it seemed that at least the fighting was over for the time being.

War Again!

At the end of World War II, the world prayed for peace. The leaders of many nations met to try to solve the problems that might lead to another world war. In Asia, the country of *Korea* had been occupied during World War II by *Japan*. After the war was over, Korea was divided into two parts. *South Korea* was occupied by United States troops, and *North Korea* was occupied by Communist troops. Each side was to help its section of Korea overcome the effects of the war years.

The United States wanted *elections* to be held with all Korean citizens voting. The Communist leaders of North Korea objected. They did not want elections to be held. They said Korea was not ready to be united under one government. Eventually the United States held elections in South Korea. *Syngman Rhee* was elected president of South Korea.

In June 1950, Korea came into the news again. An army of North Korean soldiers attacked South Korea. The *United Nations* met and decided to send troops to help South Korea. General *Douglas MacArthur* was placed in charge of the United Nations troops.

The *Korean War* lasted from 1950 to 1953. During these years, United Nations troops fought Communist North Korean troops. Sometimes it appeared that the North Koreans would win. Other times it appeared that the United Nations forces would win. In 1953, a *truce,* or cease-fire, was agreed upon. Korea was divided at the 38th parallel. Both South Korea and North Korea continued to exist.

The world learned that the United Nations troops could be called out to defend an invaded nation. The independence of South Korea was preserved.

Review Exercise

Each of the following groups describes five events that have happened since World War I. All of these events have had a big effect on our lives today. The events as they appear in each group are out of order. By writing a, b, c, d, or e next to each line, arrange the events in their proper order. The event that came first should have an "a" after it. The second event would have a "b" following it, and so on. Look back over the last unit if you need help. Each group is to be done by itself. Do not combine the four groups.

I.   The Union of Soviet Socialist Republics was formed.   _____

The Communist Revolution took place in Russia.   _____

Much of the world had a terrible depression.   _____

General Franco became dictator of Spain.   _____

President Roosevelt started his New Deal.   _____

II. Benito Mussolini set up the Fascist party in Italy.   _____

India became a free nation.   _____

The Nazi party took control of Germany.   _____

The League of Nations broke down.   _____

Germany invaded Austria.   _____

III. The Japanese bombed Pearl Harbor.   _____

Germany defeated France.   _____

Germany invaded Poland.   _____

The atomic bomb was dropped on two Japanese cities.   _____

Germany declared war on the United States.   _____

IV. NATO was formed.   _____

The United Nations was formed.   _____

Communists invaded South Korea.   _____

The Berlin Airlift began.   _____

World War II ended.   _____

Puzzle Quiz

Read each of the following clues. Place the correct answers in the spaces provided. The words are taken out of the last chapter.

1. _ _ _ _ _   K _ _ _ _

2. _ O _ _ _   _ _ _ _ _

3. R _ _ _

4. E _ _ _ _ _ _ _ _

5. _ A _ _ _ _ _ _

6. _ N _ _ _ _   _ _ _ _ _ _ _

7. _ _ _ _ _ _   W _ _

8. _ A _ _ _

9. _ R _ _ _

Clues

1. _____ _____ invaded South Korea in June 1950.

2. The U.S. occupied this country after World War II.

3. Syngman _____ was elected president of South Korea.

4. The United States wanted to hold _____ in Korea, but North Korea said no.

5. Douglas _____ led the United Nations forces in Korea.

6. This organization sent troops into South Korea.

7. The _____ _____ occurred from 1950 to 1953.

8. _____ occupied Korea during World War II.

9. A _____, or cease-fire, brought the Korean War to a close in 1953.

YEARS OF HOPE AND DISAPPOINTMENT

10

Introduction

Anyone who has ever helped fight a forest fire knows how hard it can be to control. The 1950's, 1960's, and 1970's were much like a forest fire. A new "hot spot" showed up every time another cooled down. All it took was a spark to set off a new problem.

Some of the problems were solved. Others are still hot and dangerous. Let's take a quick look at the years following the Korean War. We will examine what made the news and what importance it has for us.

The Mideast— International Hot Spot

In 1948, *Israel* became a nation. Much of the land in the new nation had once belonged to Arabs. The Arab nations around Israel wanted that land back. They also didn't agree with the *Jewish* religion. Almost as soon as Israel became a nation, the surrounding Arab nations went to war. Though the Arabs greatly outnumbered the Israelis, the war soon went in favor of Israel.

Despite such a poor beginning, the tiny country of Israel did well. Jews from all over the world came to live in Israel. Scientists introduced improved methods of growing crops in Israel's dry lands. Modern buildings and factories were built. The people prospered.

Jerusalem, old and new

None of this made the Arab nations happy. Even though they sold *oil* throughout the world, they were jealous of Israel's progress. Most people in the Arab nations lived hard lives. The *standard of living* was very poor compared with that of their new neighbor, Israel.

In 1954, *Gamal Nasser* took over the leadership of *Egypt*. As leader of this large Arab nation, he tried to make things better for the people. He tried to help both farmers and businesspeople. In 1956, he took over control of the *Suez Canal* from Britain. Great Britain and France protested. Since Egypt had also supported raids on Israel, Israel now invaded Egypt.

At the request of the *United Nations*, the invading Israeli army left Egyptian territory. Israel and her Arab neighbors once more watched each other with suspicion.

Golda Meir (1898–1978)

Golda Meir was born in Kiev, Russia on May 3, 1898. Life in Russia was hard. Golda's father took the family to the United States. Golda attended school but fought with her parents. She wanted to be a teacher. Her parents disagreed, so Golda moved to Colorado to live with her sister. She did become a teacher but is not remembered for her teaching.

After marrying in 1917, Golda and her husand moved to Palestine. Golda had become interested in Zionism. Zionism was the plan for setting up a Jewish homeland in Palestine. Golda had met David Ben-Gurion, who spoke for the Zionist movement.

In Palestine Golda and her husband lived and worked in a farm community called a *kibbutz*. Her husband did not like the kibbutz, so they eventually moved to Jerusalem. To make ends meet, Golda took in laundry because they were so poor.

They continued to work for a Jewish homeland. After World War II, Israel, a Jewish country, was created. The Arab countries hated Israel. They have fought Israel many times since World War II.

David Ben-Gurion became premier of Israel. Golda was Israel's first envoy to Russia. When she returned, she was named

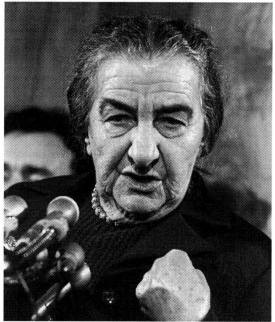

Minister of Labor and then Minister of Foreign Affairs in 1956. That year, the Arabs attacked Israel. When the war was over, Golda went to the United Nations.

Golda Meir was named premier in March 1969. She worked on Israel's national security. She also tried to find ways to have lasting peace with the Arabs.

She was premier when Egypt and Syria attacked in 1973. This was the Yom Kippur War, which Israel won quickly.

Golda Meir remained premier until 1974, when she resigned. She died in Jerusalem on December 8, 1978.

During the next eleven years, the situation didn't improve much. Finally, in 1967, the Arabs refused to let Israel use the *Gulf of Aqaba* to get to its port of *Elath*. For the third time in twenty years, war broke out. This time the war lasted six days. Israel took land from *Jordan* and Egypt. This time, however, Israel refused to give the land back. Israel kept it to protect its own borders.

The *Six-Day War* of 1967 did not end the problems between Israel and its neighbors. Again in 1973, Egypt and *Syria* were at war with Israel. When the fighting stopped, Israel had gained land. Israel and Egypt made peace quickly. Relations with Syria stayed poor.

The Mideast Continues to Make News

The end of the war between Israel and its neighbors did not mean the *Mideast* was quiet. Beginning in 1973, the Arabs started using oil to get their way. In 1973, the Arab oil *embargo* resulted in fewer shipments of oil to the United States and to other nations friendly with Israel. The embargo lasted about a year.

The Organization of Petroleum Exporting Countries (*OPEC*) began raising oil prices. A *barrel* of oil cost less than $3 in 1972. By 1978, the price had increased to about $16 a barrel. In oil-importing

nations, like the United States, this resulted in great price increases in *manufacturing, transportation*, food production, and *utilities*.

Oil wasn't the only thing that kept the Mideast in the news. *Muslims* and *Christians* began fighting in *Beirut, Lebanon*, in April of 1975. This *civil war* raged for a year and a half. Finally, other Arab nations stepped in and stopped the civil war. But the people of Lebanon are still not happy with each other, and unrest continues.

Terrorism has been a part of the Mideast for years. Many terrorist groups have grown out of Mideast troubles. One such group *invaded* the Olympic village during the 1972 *Olympics*. They took the Israeli team as *hostages*. Eleven hostages and five terrorists were killed before the day of terror ended. Airplane hijackings, bombs set to explode in public places, and kidnapping are other weapons terrorists have used.

> **Think About It:**
> Why do some people resort to terror while others do not?

When Israel became a nation, many Arabs wanted a nation or *homeland* for the *Palestinian* people. These are the people who were displaced when Israel was formed. Many acts of terrorism have been attempts to convince other nations to help form a Palestinian nation.

The *Palestine Liberation Organization* is one group that has worked for such a homeland. The *PLO*, as it is called, often took part in terrorist activities. The PLO leader, *Yasir Arafat*, has spoken about the problem before the United Nations.

Most leaders recognize the need for peace in the Mideast. In 1977, President *Sadat* of Egypt met with Prime Minister *Begin* of Israel to discuss peace. It was the first time in history that an Arab leader and a leader of Israel met to talk peace.

Peace will not be easy to achieve. It will take the best efforts of everyone in order to bring peace to the Mideast.

Modern Map of the Middle East

For each question, choose one of the four answers. You will have to use the map on page 121 to decide which answer is correct.

1. On this map Turkey appears to be which of the following?
   a) a peninsula b) an island c) a member of the Arab world d) an ally or friend of Israel

2. This country is divided into two parts by water from the Mediterranean Sea and the Black Sea.
   a) Lebanon   b) Turkey   c) Iran   d) Syria

3. Which of these countries does not border the Mediterranean Sea?
   a) Israel   b) Egypt   c) Jordan   d) Lebanon

4. What is the smallest sea shown on the map?
   a) Red Sea   b) Black Sea   c) Mediterranean Sea   d) Dead Sea

5. Israel touched three bodies of water before June 1967. Which of the following bodies of water did Israel **not** touch?
   a) Mediterranean Sea   b) Dead Sea   c) Gulf of Aqaba   d) Red Sea

6. Which of the following statements applies to Israel after the 1967 war?
   a) Its territory got smaller.
   b) Its territory got larger.
   c) It lost its boundary on the Mediterranean Sea, but gained territory.
   d) Its territory remained unchanged.

7. Israel took the most land from which of these Arab nations?
   a) Egypt   b) Jordan   c) Syria   d) Lebanon

8. Before 1967, Jerusalem was located on the border between Israel and:
   a) Egypt   b) Jordan   c) Syria   d) Lebanon

9. After the 1967 war, Jerusalem was located completely inside this country.
   a) Egypt   b) Jordan   c) Syria   d) Israel

10. Israel's port of Elath was located on this body of water.
    a) Gulf of Suez   b) Gulf of Aqaba   c) Dead Sea   d) Red Sea

11. The Suez Canal allowed ships to go from the Gulf of Suez to this body of water.
    a) Dead Sea   b) Black Sea   c) Mediterranean Sea   d) Gulf of Aqaba

12. The Gulf of Aqaba flows into this body of water.
    a) Red Sea   b) Dead Sea   c) Black Sea   d) Mediterranean Sea

13. When Israel was holding the east side of the Suez Canal, which country was holding the west side of the Canal?
    a) Egypt   b) Jordan   c) Syria   d) Lebanon

14. What Arab country borders Israel on the north?
    a) Syria   b) Jordan   c) Lebanon   d) Egypt

15. What river is used for irrigation by the Israelis before it flows into the Dead Sea?
    a) Suez River   b) Aqaba River   c) Jordan River   d) Dead River

ISRAEL AND THE NEAR EAST, 1973

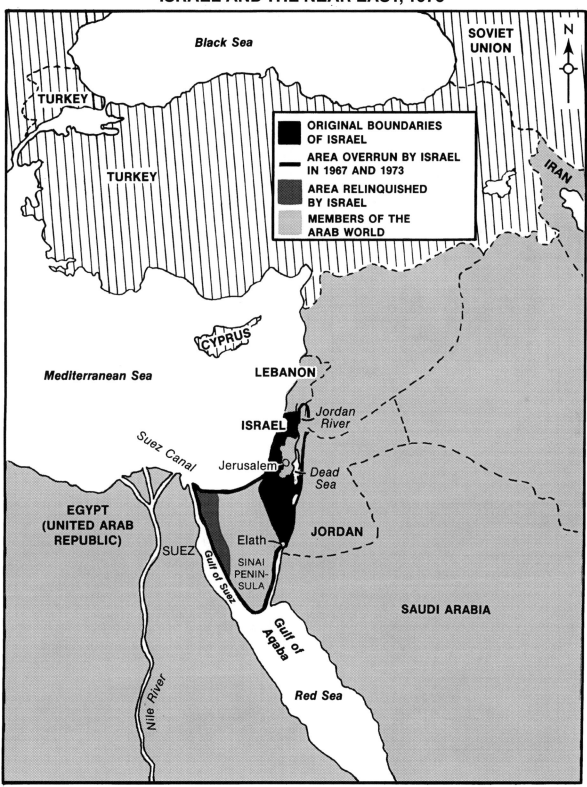

Puzzle Quiz

Read each of the puzzle clues below. Find the words or phrases in the material you just read concerning the Mideast. Then write the answers in the correct row or column of the puzzle.

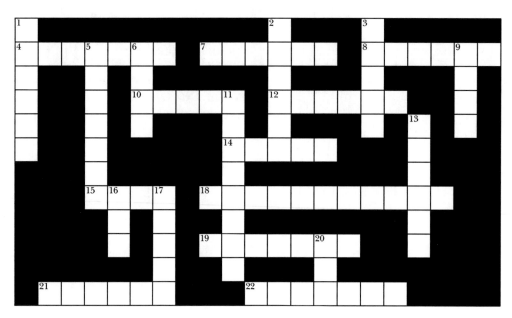

Across

4. Name for the area that includes Israel, Syria, Lebanon, Jordan
7. Jewish nation in the Mideast
8. Last name of the leader of the PLO
10. The Six-Day War began after Egypt refused to let Israel use this port.
12. The _____ War took place in 1967.
14. Arab nation that helped Egypt in 1973
15. Abbreviation for Organization of Petroleum Exporting Countries
18. The PLO wants a homeland for the _____ people.
19. Nation in which Muslims and Christians fought each other
21. Unit of measure for petroleum
22. Few Arabs are Christians. Most are _____.

Down

1. Something that is brought into a country
2. Last name of ruler who took control of Egypt in 1954
3. Egyptian president who tried to make peace with Israel in 1977
5. To halt trade with a nation; the oil _____ is an example.
6. Canal belonging to Egypt
9. Egypt, Syria, and Saudi Arabia are all _____ nations.
11. People held by terrorists
13. To take control of an airplane illegally
16. Abbreviation for Palestine Liberation Organization
17. A war is one in which two parts of a nation fight each other
20. Common name for petroleum

Communism vs. Democracy

From the end of World War II through the 1980's, there was a struggle between *communism* and *democracy*. At times this struggle was a battle of words and ideas. Sometimes the struggle was fought with bombs and bullets.

In the following pages, you will read about the events that highlighted this struggle. After you finish reading these pages, decide for yourself which side came out ahead and why. Let's begin by reading about a Communist nation located about 100 miles south of *Florida*.

Cuba

In 1898, the United States took *Cuba* from *Spain*. In 1934, Cuba was given complete *independence*. *Fulgencio Batista* gained influence in the government and eventually came to rule the nation with an iron hand. In 1959, however, *Fidel Castro* was able to take control of Cuba. The United States was happy to see Batista defeated. So were many Cubans. However, many people soon thought Castro was worse than Batista.

Fidel Castro

Castro took land belonging to American companies without paying for it. He told the world he was a *Communist*. The *Soviet Union* began to send weapons and money to Cuba. Many people began to leave Cuba. Cuban *exiles* arrived in Florida in great numbers.

In 1961, a band of these exiles invaded Cuba. They planned to retake Cuba from Castro. After they landed at the *Bay of Pigs*, everything went wrong. They had hoped a popular uprising would help them. It never happened, and the invasion failed. The United States was involved in the episode.

In the fall of 1962, United States planes photographed Soviet *missile* sites in Cuba. The missiles were aimed at the United States. The United States set up a *naval blockade* around Cuba. President *Kennedy* ordered the *Soviets* to remove their missiles. War seemed possible, but the Soviets and Cubans backed down. The missiles were taken back to the U.S.S.R.

Cuba has remained Communist. Yet its relations with Russia and the United States are changing. While the Soviets gave Castro millions of dollars worth of aid, the United States had a complete trade embargo with Cuba. While this lasted, the Cubans were not able to make their nation prosper.

However, the United States and Cuba began to get along better. For years hijackers had flown to Cuba with American planes and passengers. In 1973, Cuba agreed to punish hijackers or to return them to the United States if they had taken an American airplane. The next year President *Ford* said he felt relations with Cuba could be improved.

In 1977, Castro invited Americans to visit Cuba. It was not long before the United States and Cuba were talking about buying and selling from and to one another. Perhaps the best indication that Castro didn't make everyone like communism is that over 650,000 Cubans left Cuba after Castro took over. Most of them came to the United States. But it is important to keep in mind also that over 11 million people still live in Cuba. For many of them, life under Castro has been better than the terrible poverty they suffered before.

> **Think About It:**
> By 1999, Fidel Castro had ruled Cuba for 40 years. During that time the United States had nine presidents. How was Castro able to stay in power even as Cuba as a whole became poorer?

Uprisings Against the Communists

In June 1953, three months after *Joseph Stalin* died, workers in *East Berlin* became unhappy over working conditions. Their protest resulted in a *riot*. Over 200,000 East Germans became involved. Soviet troops crushed the protest. Sixteen East Germans died in the fighting.

Following World War II, the Soviet Union had gained control of several East European nations. One of these was *Hungary*. The young people of Hungary felt changes were needed to help their country. They wanted these changes to come quickly.

On October 24, 1956, students in Hungary began rioting against Soviet rule. The *revolt* spread through the nation. On November 4, nearly a quarter of a million Soviet troops and more than two thousand tanks attacked the students in the city of *Budapest*. In ten days the battle was over. The young Hungarians fought well, but they were no match for the trained Soviet soldiers. Pistols and bricks were no match for tanks. The Hungarian attempt at freedom was over.

In 1968, the Communist leaders of *Czechoslovakia* came close to being *overthrown* by angry citizens. Only the arrival of Soviet tanks saved the government. Students in *Warsaw, Poland*, another Communist country, rioted in support of the people of Czechoslovakia. Though the riots ended quickly, they were one more sign of unrest.

> **Think About It:**
> Many people in such nations as Hungary, Czechoslovakia, and East Germany hated communist rule. Why didn't democratic nations help these people overthrow their communist leaders? Looking back, was it a wise decision not to help?

The Cold War and the Iron Curtain

When the Soviets refused to allow Western nations to use the roads into Berlin, the *cold war* set in. The cold war went on through the 1980's. It was a war fought with words and threats for the most part. Germany was often in the center of this strange conflict.

For a few years people were allowed to go from *East Germany* into *West Germany*, and back again. But since more and more people didn't return to East Germany each year, the Soviets began refusing to let people travel between the two parts of Germany.

The English leader *Sir Winston Churchill* once said that an *"iron curtain"* divided Europe. He was right. The Soviets finally built miles of walls and barbed wire fences to keep people in the Communist part of Germany. In Berlin the wall was made of brick, concrete, and barbed wire. The *Berlin Wall* brought death to many Germans who tried to escape to freedom. It came to represent all that was wrong with communism.

Different Brands of Communism

When Stalin died in 1953, Soviet communism began to change. The leaders who followed Stalin weren't as harsh as he had been. These new leaders were less likely to use war. They depended on *propaganda*, or well-chosen words designed to spread their ideas.

As we have seen, all was not well in the Communist nations. Even before the death of Stalin, *Yugoslavia* was beginning to have Communist ideas of its own. Its leader, *Marshal Tito*, was an independent-minded Communist *dictator.* Often he refused to take orders from the Soviet Union. His people backed him and he remained their leader, in spite of what Soviet Communists said.

The biggest problem area for world communism was *China.* China has the largest population of any Communist country. *Chairman Mao Tse-tung* was the leader of the *People's Republic of China.* He felt the world would turn to communism only through armed force. The Soviets hoped other people would choose to join their movement. This difference of opinion between the two giant Communist nations resulted in trouble. Several border fights took place between Chinese and Soviet troops. Both nations aimed missiles at each other. The two nations distrusted each other a great deal.

In October 1971, the *United Nations* voted for the first time to admit the People's Republic of China to the UN. Since 1945, the *Republic of China* had been a UN member. Today all that is left of the Republic of China is the island of *Taiwan.* When the UN admitted Communist China, it threw out the Taiwan Chinese.

In an effort to improve relations between the United States and mainland China, President *Nixon* visited *Beijing* and other Chinese cities in 1972. Nixon was the first U.S. president to visit the People's Republic of China. He called his trip a *"journey of peace."*

Chairman Mao Tse-tung, leader of China since the Communists took over in 1949, died in September 1976. After his death, new leaders took over the country. Some of Mao's friends and even his wife became unpopular.

War in Vietnam

Many nations gave up their colonies peacefully after World War II. Others, such as France, did not. *French Indochina* had been divided into the new nations of *Laos, Cambodia*, and *Vietnam.* Because of a lack of understanding, France went to war with Vietnam on December 9, 1946. Twenty-five years later, that war was still going on. France, however, was no longer fighting. Instead, the United States was taking part. How did this happen?

Ho Chi Minh led the people of Vietnam against France. His armies soon began to get the better of the French forces. In May 1954, the French were defeated in a terrible battle. Vietnam became two nations, *North Vietnam* and *South Vietnam.* North Vietnam, under the leadership of Ho Chi Minh, was Communist. Those in power in South Vietnam did not want to be ruled by the Communists. They asked the United States for help to train an army.

In 1955, President *Eisenhower* sent men to help train the army of South Vietnam. One thing led to another. By 1959, American *advisers* had been killed by North Vietnamese soldiers. President *Kennedy* promised to help South Vietnam fight communism. By the end of 1963, there were 15,000 Americans in Vietnam.

Soldiers in training

Then things began to get worse. In 1964, it was claimed that two United States ships had been attacked in the *Gulf of Tonkin.* President *Johnson* used this "attack" as a reason to start bombing North Vietnam. Three years later, there were over half a million American troops in Vietnam. The cost of the war was over $25 billion a year.

To try to end the war, the United States stopped most of its bombing of North Vietnam. President Nixon eventually started to bring American troops home. Over 46,000 American soldiers were killed in Vietnam. The war was the longest the United States had ever fought. It was also one of the most expensive. Its total cost was almost $141 billion. Many Americans felt we should never have become involved. Almost everyone wanted it to end.

Think About It:
Thousands of American troops returned from the Vietnam War suffering from terrible battle injuries and stress. What changes did these injured war veterans bring to our daily lives?

In January 1969, peace talks opened in *Paris.* They seemed to do little good. The next year U.S. and South Vietnamese troops invaded *Cambodia*, one of Vietnam's neighbors. The troops destroyed Communist supply bases in Cambodia.

In the United States, students and other citizens protested the war in Vietnam and the attacks on Cambodia. In 1971, President Nixon sent *Henry Kissinger* to begin secret peace talks with the leaders of North Vietnam. The secret talks seemed to work. By August 1972, United States *combat* troops were out of Vietnam. In January 1973, a peace agreement was signed. Hundreds of American prisoners of war were released by the Communists. Over 1,000 missing American troops (MIA's) were never located, however.

In June 1976, the two parts of Vietnam officially formed one nation. The government was almost completely in the hands of Communist leaders from North Vietnam.

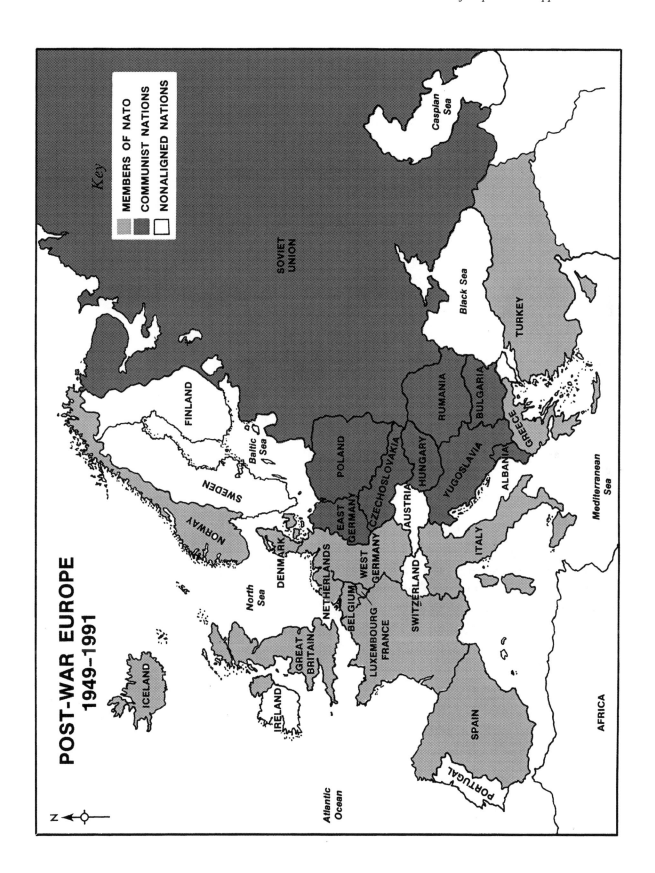

POST-WAR EUROPE
1949–1991

Key

MEMBERS OF NATO
COMMUNIST NATIONS
NONALIGNED NATIONS

Postwar Europe Puzzle Quiz

Read each clue carefully. Find the country or body of water described on the map of postwar Europe on page 127. Write the answer to each clue in the puzzle spaces on page 129. Make sure each answer fits the puzzle exactly.

Across

1. This is the largest country on the continent of Europe.
4. This small country is south of the Netherlands and borders France.
6. This Communist country is south of the Soviet Union on the Black Sea.
7. This Communist country is almost as long as Italy and is separated from Italy by water.
9. This NATO pact nation extends farther north than any other.
13. This Communist country is south of Poland and north of both Austria and Hungary.
15. This nonaligned nation is found east of Switzerland and west of Hungary.
17. This country is found on the west coast of Europe, south of Great Britain.
18. This is the largest island off the west coast of Europe.
23. This small body of water is south of both Sweden and Finland and north of Poland and East Germany.
25. This country borders Belgium and West Germany. It is also on the North Sea.
27. This far north, nonaligned nation borders the Soviet Union.
28. This country, south of France, borders both the Mediterranean Sea and the Atlantic Ocean.
29. This NATO pact nation country is south of Yugoslavia on the Mediterranean Sea.

Down

1. This nonaligned nation is located between Norway and Finland.
2. A narrow channel of water divides this country into two parts. The largest part of this country is south of the Black Sea.
3. This country looks like a boot that is sticking into the Mediterranean Sea.
4. This Communist nation lies between Rumania and Turkey.
5. This sea is located south of Europe. It has the longest name of any sea on the map.
8. This small Communist country lies south of Yugoslavia and north of Greece.
10. This small country is on a peninsula between the North Sea and the Baltic Sea.
11. This sea is east of Great Britain and west of Norway.
12. This country borders the Atlantic Ocean and shares a peninsula with Spain.
14. This is the Communist part of Germany. Use both words and don't skip a blank.
16. This small, nonaligned country borders Italy on the north and France on the east.
19. This body of water is surrounded by the Soviet Union, Turkey, Rumania, and Bulgaria. Use both words.

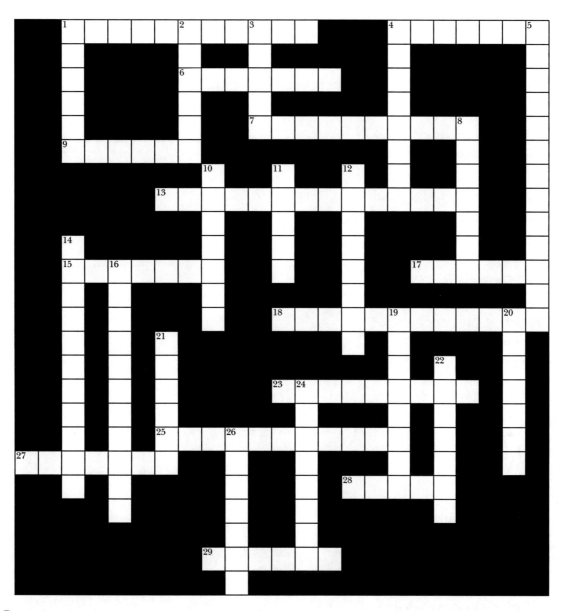

Down *(continued)*

20. This nonaligned island nation lies west of the island of Great Britain.
21. This country is between the Soviet Union and East Germany.
22. The country of West _____ borders France on the east.
24. This ocean is located off the west coast of the continent of Europe.
26. This Communist country is located north of Yugoslavia and south of Czechoslovakia.

Puzzle Quiz

Solve the puzzle below with words used in the pages you have just read on communism vs. democracy. The answer to each clue is in bold italics in the text. Be sure each answer you choose fits the puzzle spaces exactly.

1. A war of words and threats

   C _ _ _   _ _ _ _

2. U.S. state closest to Cuba

   _ _ O _ _ _ _ _

3. Leader of North Vietnam during the war

   _ _   _ _ _   M _ _ _

4. Chinese Communist who died in 1976

   M _ _   _ _ _ - _ _ _ _

5. Political system of China and Russia

   _ _ _ _ U _ _ _ _

6. First U.S. president to visit Communist China

   N _ _ _ _

7. People driven from their homeland

   _ _ I _ _ _

8. _____ Germany was Communist.

   _ _ S _

9. Soviet _____ sites were in Cuba in 1962.

   M _ _ _ _ _ _ _

10. U.S. president who sent advisers to South Vietnam

    _ _ S _ _ _ _ _ _ _

11. Fidel _____ rules Cuba.

    _ _ _ T _ _

12. A wall divided this German city

    _ _ R _ _ _

13. Hungarian city invaded by Soviets in 1956

    _ U _ _ _ _ _ _

14. Henry _____ held secret peace talks in 1971.

    _ _ _ _ _ G _ _

15. Students in _____ revolted in 1956.

    _ _ _ G _ _ _

16. Name for an uprising

    _ _ _ _ L _

17. President who had Cuba blockaded

    _ E _ _ _ _ _

18. City where Vietnam peace talks were held

    _ _ _ _ S

19. Island controlled by the Republic of China

        _ _ _ W _ _

20. Communist nation with the largest population

        _ _ I _ _

21. U.S. ships were "attacked" in the Gulf of _____.

        T _ _ _ _ _ _

22. French _____ was divided into Laos, Cambodia, and Vietnam.

        _ _ _ _ _ H _ _ _

23. Any ruler with total power

        D _ _ _ _ _ _ _

24. America's longest war was in _____.

        _ _ E _ _ _ _

25. Nation attacked by U.S. and South Vietnamese troops in 1970

        _ _ M _ _ _ _ _

26. President who began bombing North Vietnam

        _ O _ _ _ _ _

27. Churchill said an iron _____ divided Europe.

        C _ _ _ _ _ _

28. Polish city where students rioted

        _ _ R _ _ _

29. Russian leader who died in 1953

        _ _ A _ _ _

30. Communist nation ruled by Castro

        C _ _ _

31. Nation ruled by Tito

        Y _ _ _ _ _ _ _ _

A TIME
OF CHANGE
AND PROGRESS

11

Introduction

Change and progress came in many forms. New nations were carved from old ones. Old nations took new names and different forms of government. European rule ended in Africa.

In Europe, the nations not under Communist rule began to work together. Oil was discovered under the North Sea. Some nations no longer had to depend on OPEC for their fuel.

The space age advanced. The U.S.S.R. won the race to put a satellite and then a man into orbit. But only U.S. astronauts walked on the moon.

Open-heart surgery became common. Heart, kidney, and liver transplants replaced damaged organs with healthy ones.

Television, computers, and laser beams changed the way we communicate—and play!

With advances came problems. Air pollution hurt cities and entire nations. Water pollution turned some rivers into open sewers. Some countries destroyed their rain forest. Others were victims of acid rain. Humans may be destroying the ozone layer of the atmosphere and changing the earth's weather.

Trouble in India, Pakistan, and Bangladesh

In 1947, the British stopped ruling India. The people of India found they could not unite under one government. Many of the people were *Hindus*. Many others were *Muslims*. In August 1947, India was divided into two nations. The Muslims ruled the new nation of *Pakistan*. The Hindus controlled India.

Pakistan was split into two parts 900 miles away from each other. India was in the middle. This led to problems.

The great Indian leader *Mohandas Gandhi* was *assassinated* in January 1948. His death caused great unrest in both nations. During the years that followed, India and Pakistan were ready for war several times. Usually, their arguments were over small bits of land.

In 1962, Chinese Communist troops invaded India. Fear of a Communist takeover helped India and Pakistan get along better for a few years. Then, in December 1971, war broke out between India and Pakistan. As a result of the war, the eastern part of Pakistan became a new nation, Bangladesh.

These three neighboring nations all have problems. Too many people, too little food, floods, and terrible storms have caused difficulties. *Political* troubles have also caused problems.

Indira Gandhi (1917–1984)

Indira Gandhi was the daughter of Jawaharlal Nehru. She was born in India in 1917. Her father, Nehru, worked for India's independence from Great Britain. Because of this, Nehru spent many years in prison.

Indira was educated both in India and at Oxford University in England. In 1942, she married Feroz Gandhi, who died in 1960.

After India's independence from Great Britain in 1947, Nehru became prime minister. Indira helped her father during his years as prime minister. She became more and more interested in politics. She belonged to the Congress party and began to serve on political committees.

When Nehru died in 1964, Indira was appointed Minister of Information and Broadcasting. She was part of the cabinet of Shastri, the new prime minister.

In 1966, Mrs. Gandhi was made prime minister of India. She was faced with many problems, including strikes. Her own party was seriously divided. The nation was divided as well. It was her job to build a united India.

Mrs. Gandhi was re-elected in 1971. In mid-1975 she was charged with illegal election practices during the 1971 election. The election was declared null and void. Many people wanted her to resign. She reacted harshly. She declared a state of emergency. Police were given the power to arrest and hold people in jail without trial. Newspapers were censored. They were not allowed to print anything against the government.

Mrs. Gandhi and many others in her party felt India's population was too large. They passed birth control measures to reduce the growth of India's population. Many people objected to this government interference.

Many people resented Sanjay, Mrs. Gandhi's son. They felt he had too much power over his mother and the people.

Many Indians changed their opinion of Mrs. Gandhi. They wondered if India was still a democracy. As a result, Mrs. Gandhi and her party were voted out of power in early 1977.

In 1980, Mrs. Gandhi again became prime minister. Again she tried to unite India. Many people feared and hated her. In June 1984, the government put down a Sikh uprising in the Indian state of Punjab. Sikhs are very strict Hindus. During this action, an assault on the Golden Temple took place. The Golden Temple is the holiest Sikh shrine. Because of this Mrs. Gandhi was shot and killed on October 31, 1984. The killers were two of her Sikh bodyguards.

Think About It:

Mrs. Gandhi was defeated in the 1977 election. Three years later she was re-elected in a landslide victory. What events might have caused voters in India to do this?

Asia in 1980

Read each of the questions below. Underline the correct answer. You may use the map of Asia provided on page 135.

1. Which of these four oceans does not border Asia?
   a) Arctic   b) Atlantic   c) Indian   d) Pacific

2. Which nation controlled the most land in Asia in 1980?
   a) Soviet Union   b) China   c) Mongolia   d) India

3. What nation was divided by war into two countries?
   a) Japan   b) Malaysia   c) Myanmar (Burma)   d) Korea

4. These two nations share one island.
   a) Malaysia and Indonesia   c) Sri Lanka and Indonesia
   b) Philippines and Taiwan

5. Which nation appears to be the smallest on your map?
   a) Sri Lanka   b) Bhutan   c) Japan   d) Nepal

6. This nation is totally surrounded by the Soviet Union and China.
   a) Bhutan   b) Afghanistan   c) Laos   d) Mongolia

7. Name the two nations shown on the map that consist of only one island each.
   a) Taiwan and Sri Lanka   c) Japan and Philippines
   b) Nepal and Bangladesh

8. This nation has the longest coastline in Asia.
   a) China   b) India   c) Pakistan   d) Soviet Union

9. The only one of these countries to have a seacoast is:
   a) Afghanistan   b) Laos   c) Cambodia   d) Nepal

10. How many major islands make up the nation of Japan?
    a) one   b) three   c) four   d) six

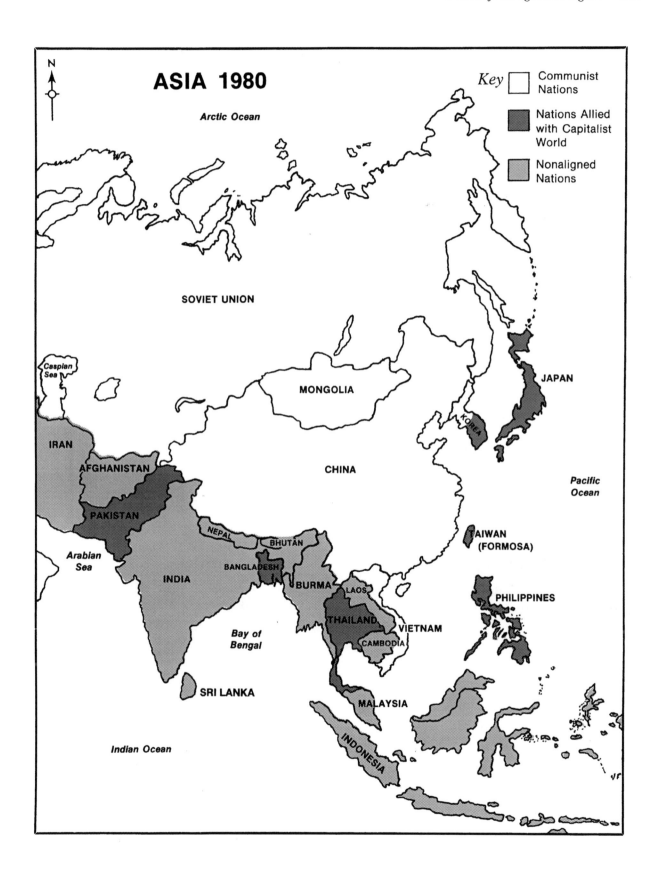

ASIA 1980

Key Communist Nations

Nations Allied with Capitalist World

Nonaligned Nations

N

Arctic Ocean

SOVIET UNION

Caspian Sea

MONGOLIA

JAPAN

KOREA

IRAN

AFGHANISTAN

CHINA

Pacific Ocean

PAKISTAN

NEPAL

BHUTAN

Arabian Sea

BANGLADESH

TAIWAN (FORMOSA)

INDIA

BURMA

LAOS

PHILIPPINES

THAILAND

VIETNAM

Bay of Bengal

CAMBODIA

SRI LANKA

MALAYSIA

Indian Ocean

INDONESIA

The European Common Market and North Sea Oil

The small nations of Europe could not compete with large *industrial* nations such as the United States. They needed to unite. The first step toward forming a united Europe came in 1949. The tiny countries of Belgium, the Netherlands, and Luxembourg formed a *trading community*. It was known as *Benelux*. In 1952, the *European Coal and Steel Community* was formed to help *trade* in Europe. Fourteen nations joined.

By 1957, the *European Economic Community*, or *Common Market*, came into being. The idea behind the Common Market was that one member would not tax products of another member. This lowered prices and encouraged member nations to buy from other Common Market countries.

In 1961, *Great Britain* tried to join the Common Market. Great Britain traded heavily with the United States and the *British Commonwealth*. *Charles de Gaulle* of *France* kept Great Britain out of the Common Market.

After World War II, France had a hard time. It could not agree on a government. Finally, in 1958, Charles de Gaulle, a war hero, became president. De Gaulle was able to help France recover.

France developed atomic weapons. This gave it world power. It was a major member of the Common Market. In 1966, France withdrew from the military part of NATO and ordered the United States to take its defense forces out of France. De Gaulle didn't want any other nation giving orders to France.

After de Gaulle's death in 1970, many things changed. On January 1, 1973, Great Britain became a Common Market member. Ireland and Denmark also joined.

European nations had to import petroleum from other places. This meant that European nations were harmed by an oil embargo and rising oil prices. In 1969, a major oil discovery was made beneath the North Sea.

The need for oil was great. Oil wells were drilled in spite of deep water, high tides, and storms. By 1978, North Sea oil was supplying about half of Great Britain's needs. Only a few years before, Great Britain had imported all its oil.

North Sea oil rig

Great Britain's oil helped make it a valuable Common Market member. Ideas such as the Common Market helped small European nations grow stronger. At the end of the twentieth century the ideal of a true European community is coming closer. A common currency, few border restrictions, and a tunnel linking Great Britain to the continent are already in place.

Think About It:
The Arab oil embargo hurt the economies of many nations. How did the fear of future oil embargoes actually help some nations?

Political Problems and Changes in Western Europe

Not all of Western Europe's problems and changes had to do with trade and oil. Politics have always been important in Europe. At the end of World War II, one dictator still ruled. He was General *Francisco Franco*. Franco ruled Spain with an iron hand for 36 years. His death in November 1975 gave the people of Spain a chance to say what sort of government they wanted. In June 1977, Spain held its first free elections since before World War II.

In *Northern Ireland* things were not good. Northern Ireland, or Ulster, was formed as a British colony in the 1700's. The rest of Ireland revolted from English oppression in 1916 and became a nation. It is mostly *Roman Catholic*. Northern Ireland decided to remain a part of the *United Kingdom*. Most of the people in Northern Ireland are *Protestant*. It stayed loyal to Great Britain, also largely a Protestant nation. Some people wanted Northern Ireland to be a part of Ireland. They formed the *Irish Republican Army*, or the *IRA*. The IRA was declared illegal but continued to exist as a secret organization.

These religious differences caused many problems in Northern Ireland. Roman Catholics claimed they were discriminated against by the Protestants. In 1969, violence began. British troops arrived to keep order. The IRA began a *guerrilla* war against the soldiers. As more soldiers were killed, the situation got worse. Special laws were passed to punish IRA members. Suspected members of the IRA were jailed. The killing went on.

The British government took over the rule of Northern Ireland. This did not please either Catholics or Protestants. Innocent *civilians* died in bombings and shootings. IRA members set bombs in public places in England. English people were killed and injured, even though they had no active part in the problems in Northern Ireland.

British troops remained and the violence went on. It became obvious the problems in Northern Ireland were political and social, not just religious. In 1977, the Nobel Peace Prize went to two women who organized civilians on both sides to work toward peace together. But the violence did not end.

Think About It:
The Northern Ireland 'Troubles' caused thousands of deaths. All these deaths did not change the way many citizens felt about other citizens. What is needed to bring two sides together to agree to peace?

Puzzle Quiz

Each of the clues below is followed by a group of scrambled letters. Unscramble these letters to find the answer to each clue. The answers are found in the three sections on India and Europe you have just read.

1. Last name of the great Indian leader who was killed in 1948   handig
2. European trading community formed in 1949   xenuleb
3. Nation once ruled by Charles de Gaulle   rafcen
4. Location of an important 1969 oil discovery   rthno ase
5. Part of the United Kingdom where much killing has taken place   renronht leirdan
6. Abbreviation for the North Atlantic Treaty Organization   TOAN
7. Last name of the European dictator who died in 1975   arnofc
8. Nation formed in 1947 from parts of India   kastipna
9. Informal warfare is called _____ war.   reruligal
10. The European Coal and _____ Community was organized in 1952.   etles
11. The IRA is the _____ Republican Army.   riihs
12. Religious group that controls much of India   dinuh
13. First name of the Indian prime minister who ruled from 1966 until 1977   ridani
14. Common name for the European Economic Community   momonc karmet
15. Another word for oil   torlepmeu
16. People who are not in the military   viilicnas
17. Nation formed from eastern Pakistan   galnabsehd
18. Nation once ruled by General Franco   pinas
19. Religion of majority in Northern Ireland   stnatsetpro
20. Word meaning buying and selling among nations   retda

The Space Age Begins

On October 4, 1957, the Soviet Union put *Sputnik I* into *orbit* around the earth. The *satellite* weighed 184 pounds. It traveled about 18,000 miles per hour. A month later *Sputnik II* went into orbit. It weighed 1,120 pounds and carried a small dog named *Laika*.

The following January the United States put its own satellite into orbit. It was called *Explorer I* and weighed less than 20 pounds. In March, the United States orbited *Vanguard I*, which was even smaller than *Explorer I*.

In 1959, the Soviets aimed for the moon. In January, *Luna I* passed the moon on its way to the sun. The next September *Luna II* crashed into the moon. In October, *Luna III* took pictures of the dark side of the moon and radioed them back to earth. The Soviets were leaders in the space race.

Satellite

The next year space satellites came into their own. *Tiros I* helped in *weather* forecasting. *Echo I* was the first U.S. *communications* satellite.

On April 12, 1961, Major *Yuri Gagarin* orbited the earth once in a Soviet satellite. In May, America's first *astronaut*, Commander *Alan B. Shephard, Jr.*, rode *Freedom 7* to a height of 116 miles. He did not orbit the earth. In August a Soviet astronaut orbited the earth 17 times. The Soviets still led in the space race.

Astronaut
John Glenn

It wasn't until February 20, 1962, that an American orbited the earth. Colonel *John H. Glenn* circled the earth three times in *Friendship 7*.

In July, 1962, *Telstar I* was launched as a communications satellite. Radio, TV, and telephone signals were bounced off the satellite. Communications were faster between Europe and the United States. For the first time, Americans could see live TV from Europe.

The following year the Soviet Union scored another space first. The first woman in space orbited the earth 48 times. In 1964, the Soviets sent a three-person craft into orbit.

Think About It:

The space race between the United States and the Soviet Union seemed very important. Why was the race to be first and best so important during this time in history?

Space probes and earth satellites became routine. In 1965 the *Early Bird* communications satellite began orbiting the earth once every 24 hours. This speed kept it always above the same spot on earth to handle telephone and TV communications. In July 1965, *Mariner IV* sent back TV pictures of Mars. Then in December, *Gemini 6* and *Gemini 7* flew to within one foot of each other. It was the first space *rendezvous*.

In the following years moon probes, space *dockings*, and Venus probes followed. On December 27, 1968, *Apollo 8* and three U.S. astronauts orbited the moon. *Apollo 11* carried the first people to the moon July 20, 1969. *Lunar* landing *module Eagle* let Americans *Neil Armstrong* and *Edwin Aldrin* step onto the moon. At last the United States was leader in the space race.

In 1971, American astronauts rode on the moon in a lunar rover. The same year, the Soviets landed a space probe on Mars.

American and Soviet astronauts linked together in space in 1975 to visit and share meals. Thoughts turned toward orbiting space stations and orbiting *solar collectors*.

Were there things that could be done in space to help humanity here on earth?

In January 1978, a crewless Soviet supply *capsule* docked at the *Salyut 6* space station. Two days later a Soviet satellite powered by radioactive material fell from orbit. It burned up in the atmosphere over Canada. Within a few days the world saw both progress and failure in space exploration.

> **Think About It:**
> Satellites and other space material usually burn up if they fall from orbit. Why are pieces of "space junk" considered dangerous when they stay in orbit?

Puzzle Quiz

Look back over the material you just read about the space age. Find the word that correctly fills each of the following blanks. Write that word in the blank.

1. An _____ is a path in space around the earth.

2. A _____ is a space vehicle that orbits the earth.

3. An _____ is a person who travels in space.

4. The dog _____ was the first space traveler.

5. John _____ was the first American to orbit the earth.

6. In 1965, _____ *IV* sent back pictures of Mars.

7. The _____ was the first lunar landing module.

8. _____ *I* was the first satellite placed in orbit.

9. Our first weather satellite was _____ *I*.

10. Yuri _____ was the first person to orbit the earth.

11. _____ *I* was the first privately built communications satellite.

12. Alan _____ was America's first astronaut.

13. _____ *6* was the first space station supplied by a crewless space capsule.

14. America's first satellite was _____ *I*.

15. _____ *11* carried the first people to land on the moon.

16. The first human-made object to reach the moon was _____ *II.*

17. The first U.S. communications satellite was _____ *I.*

18. In 1965, _____ *7* made 220 orbits around the earth.

Now find each of the above answers in the letter maze on page 141. Circle each answer as you find it. Answers in the maze are written backwards and forwards. They may be written vertically, horizontally, or diagonally.

```
E   D   R   A   P   E   H   S   P   U   T   O   S

T   U   A   N   O   R   T   S   A   E   A   G   P

I   L   A   R   E   R   O   L   P   X   E   E   U

L   A   U   K   O   R   B   I   T   C   A   T   T

L   P   I   N   I   M   E   G   H   G   L   U   N

E   O   O   T   A   A   E   O   L   L   A   Y   I

T   L   R   A   T   S   L   E   T   E   L   L   K

A   L   N   I   R   A   G   A   G   N   U   A   O

S   O   M   A   R   I   N   E   R   N   N   S   E
```

Redrawing the Map of Africa

The modern *independence movement* in Africa began on March 6, 1957. On that date the little nation of *Ghana* became self-governing. It joined the British Commonwealth of Nations. After that, some nations became free with little effort. Others had to struggle violently to gain freedom. Some nations became free and then could not keep peace within their own borders.

Many Africans lacked a formal education. They had few of the skills needed to run a nation in an industrialized world. Doctors, teachers, and engineers were scarce. Unrest was common in much of Africa.

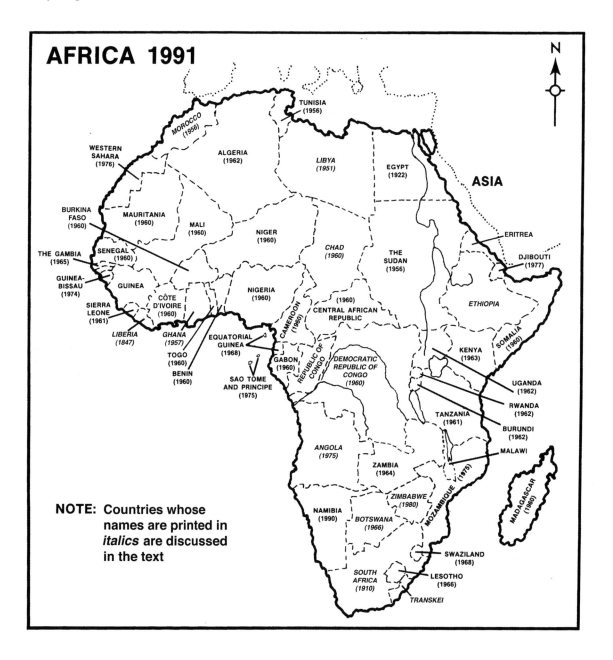

AFRICA 1991

N

TUNISIA (1956)

MOROCCO (1956)

WESTERN SAHARA (1976)

ALGERIA (1962)

LIBYA (1951)

EGYPT (1922)

ASIA

BURKINA FASO (1960)

MAURITANIA (1960)

MALI (1960)

NIGER (1960)

CHAD (1960)

THE SUDAN (1956)

ERITREA

THE GAMBIA (1965)

SENEGAL (1960)

DJIBOUTI (1977)

GUINEA-BISSAU (1974)

GUINEA

NIGERIA (1960)

(1960)
CENTRAL AFRICAN REPUBLIC

ETHIOPIA

SIERRA LEONE (1961)

CÔTE D'IVOIRE (1960)

CAMEROON (1960)

LIBERIA (1847)

GHANA (1957)

EQUATORIAL GUINEA (1968)

GABON (1960)

REPUBLIC OF CONGO

DEMOCRATIC REPUBLIC OF CONGO (1960)

KENYA (1963)

SOMALIA (1960)

TOGO (1960)

BENIN (1960)

SAO TOME AND PRINCIPE (1975)

UGANDA (1962)

RWANDA (1962)

TANZANIA (1961)

BURUNDI (1962)

ANGOLA (1975)

MALAWI

ZAMBIA (1964)

MOZAMBIQUE (1975)

MADAGASCAR (1960)

ZIMBABWE (1980)

NAMIBIA (1990)

BOTSWANA (1966)

SWAZILAND (1968)

SOUTH AFRICA (1910)

LESOTHO (1966)

TRANSKEI

NOTE: Countries whose names are printed in *italics* are discussed in the text

Ethiopia

Ethiopia was one of the oldest kingdoms in the world. It was an *independent* nation while much of Africa was controlled by European nations. Emperor *Haile Selassie* ruled Ethiopia from 1930 until 1973, except when it was taken over by Italy before World War II.

Haile Selassie allowed no political parties for years. He did try, however, to make Ethiopia a modern nation. Elections were finally held in 1957 to elect a *Parliament.* Ethiopia tried to become a leader among African nations. Great amounts of U.S. aid went to Ethiopia in the 1960's.

In 1960, some Ethiopians tried to get rid of Selassie. The following years saw more unrest. In 1973, a *famine* killed 100,000 people in Ethiopia. The next year an army *mutiny,* strikes, and student riots brought an end to Selassie's rule. Sixty of his officals were executed. Selassie was allowed to live.

In the following years various tribes fought the new government. Arab nations helped those groups. Ethiopia accepted aid from the *Soviet Union* and was for a while a communist state. In 1977, its neighbor, *Somalia,* lost a short border war with Ethiopia.

Zaire and Angola

Some African nations became independent at the cost of many lives. A number of nations had to fight to remain independent. *Zaire* (now called the *Democratic Republic of Congo*) and *Angola* are two African nations in which many lives were lost.

Zaire was once a *colony* controlled by *Belgium.* It was called the *Belgian Congo.* When it was given its independence in 1960, fight-

ing broke out. United Nations troops came into Zaire to prevent *civil war.* These troops stayed until 1964. Soon after the UN troops left, *rebels* attacked government forces. The government hired foreign soldiers to help fight the rebels. By the end of 1964, Belgium sent paratroops to rescue hostages held by the rebels.

The Zaire government tried to improve the nation and make it completely African. Citizens were told to take African names. Foreign businesses were sold to citizens of Zaire. In 1975, the price of Zaire's main *export, copper,* fell. Zaire went into debt. The nation's *economy* began to suffer. By 1977, the Zaire government asked foreign business owners to return to Zaire.

Think About It:
Zaire wanted to become completely African. Would this have been possible if the price of copper had not fallen?

Zaire's neighbor, Angola, was a colony of *Portugal.* From 1961 until 1974, a guerrilla war for independence went on. In 1974, Portugal offered independence to Angola. Almost at once violence broke out. Each of Angola's three main groups wanted to control the new nation. When independence came in 1975, most of Angola was under the control of the *Popular Movement.* This group was aided by Soviet advisers. Fifteen thousand *Cuban* troops also helped in the civil war.

More Cuban troops came to Angola. Communist soldiers from East Germany were there as well. Cubans trained soldiers who were going to invade Zaire. Angola hoped to capture Zaire's copper mines. With the help of soldiers flown from *Morocco,* Zaire was able to fight off the invasion.

South Africa and Rhodesia/Zimbabwe

The modern history of Africa was a history of white colonists ruling black natives. In most of Africa this changed during the 1960's and 1970's. Two nations of Africa still continued to have racial problems.

In *South Africa,* about four million white people controlled the government. About five times that many nonwhites had little to say about their government. This nation had a strict *segregation* policy called *apartheid.*

By 1959, the government of South Africa began setting aside land for the *Bantu* people. They make up much of South Africa's nonwhite population. By 1974, ten such areas had been set up. In 1976, the first such area, called *Transkei,* became independent. That same year 600 people died in riots protesting apartheid.

In 1977, many blacks were arrested because they opposed the government. So were whites who favored giving blacks equal rights. World opinion favored equal rights for all.

Rhodesia (now *Zimbabwe* and *Zambia*) was another African nation with racial problems.

Its 1961 constitution gave voting rights only to white citizens. In 1965, Rhodesian Prime Minister *Ian Smith* declared the nation's independence. *Great Britain* asked Rhodesia to allow its black citizens to vote. Many nations refused to trade with Rhodesia in an effort to force the government to accept black rule.

A new constitution was accepted in 1970. It had a provision that voters had to pay certain amounts of *income tax* in order to vote. This kept most blacks from voting due to their low incomes. Beginning in 1972, black guerrilla forces fought the Rhodesian army. By 1977, neighboring *Mozambique* was helping the guerrillas.

Both the United States and Great Britain tried to persuade Prime Minister Smith to change his thinking.

With both Rhodesia and South Africa, old forms of government did not change when Great Britain no longer controlled the governments.

Think About It:

The white governments in Rhodesia and South Africa tried to keep nonwhite citizens from voting. Why was voting so important to both groups?

Puzzle Quiz

Each clue below and on the following page refers to a word you read in the section on Africa. Choose your answers from the words in bold italics in the text. Be certain each answer you select fits the puzzle spaces exactly.

1. Nation once part of Rhodesia   __ I __ __ __ __ __ __ __

2. Nation that became independent in 1957   __ __ __ N __

3. Nation in which most blacks could not vote   __ __ __ D __ __ __ __

4. One of Africa's oldest independent nations   E __ __ __ __ __ __ __ __

5. Send goods out of a country   __ __ P __ __ __ __

6. Those fighting the government   __ E __ __ __ __ __

7. Self-governing   __ N __ __ __ __ __ __ __ __

8. Segregation in South Africa   __ __ __ __ __ __ __ __ D

9. Haile _____ rule Ethiopia for many years.   __ E __ __ __ __ __ __

10. Refusal of soldiers to obey orders   __ __ __ __ N __

11. Angola was a colony of _____.   __ __ __ T __ __ __ __

12. Nation helped by Cuban troops   A __ __ __ __ __ __

13. Great shortage of food   F __ __ __ __ __

14. Independent area for the Bantu in South Africa   __ R __ __ __ __ __ __

15. Tax Rhodesians had to pay to be eligible to vote   I __ __ __ __ __ __

16. War within a nation is _____ war.   C __ __ __ __

17. Nation fighting with Ethiopia in 1977   __ __ __ A __ __ __

18. Distant land controlled by another nation   __ __ __ __ N __

19. Major tribe in South Africa   _ _ N _ _

20. Nation helping
    Rhodesian geurrillas   _ _ _ A _ _ _ _ _ _

21. Ethiopia was ruled by
    _____ in World War II.   _ T _ _ _

22. Nation that once
    controlled Zaire   _ _ _ _ I _ _

23. Zaire's major export   _ O _ _ _ _

24. Governing body   _ _ _ _ _ _ _ N _

25. Last name of Rhodesia's
    last white prime minister   S _ _ _ _

New Nations With Old Problems

Life in many parts of Africa has always been a struggle for survival. *Drought*, or lack of enough rain to grow crops, is a constant fear for the people of many African nations.

In 1983, the United Nations reported that 22 African nations faced starvation. Ethiopia, Ghana, Chad, and Mozambique were worst off.

The following year, a huge foreign aid program began. It was to help the starving in Ethiopia. Not all of Ethiopia's food problems came from failed crops. Much of the starvation was caused by the nation's government.

A civil war was being fought in Ethiopia. The *Marxist* government forced millions of people to move from their homes. What food was available was given to those who supported the government. Food was used as a weapon.

Chad was another nation in which fighting added to the problems of famine. In 1983,

France sent troops to help Chad fight *rebel* soldiers. The rebels were backed by *Libya*, which wanted to control Chad. The fighting in Chad continued off and on for years.

The expansion of *desert* land in Africa gets worse each year. Most of the people burn wood for cooking and heat. Women and children destroy trees and shrubs for fuel. Once these plants are killed, the land near deserts becomes desert itself.

Another cause of the expanding desert is that livestock *overgraze* the land. They destroy grass and edible plants. When this happens, the desert expands.

Africa's *population* is increasing rapidly. Large families are common. The need for food puts demands on the land. Each year millions of acres are destroyed.

Insects have hurt Africa for thousands of years. Even modern pesticides have not killed swarms of *locusts*. Many miles across, these swarms completely eat a year's crops in an area.

The lack of education is serious. *Illiteracy*, or being unable to read, makes learning far more difficult. In today's world, people who cannot learn may lead terrible lives.

Some nations, like Kenya, are trying to save their wildlife. Meanwhile, cattle raisers want grazing land for their animals. They see no reason to preserve rhinos and elephants while their herds go hungry.

Some groups of people are suffering. The *Bushmen*, who have lived for centuries in harsh, dry lands, are crowded by expanding populations.

Many Africans moved from the country to the cities. They have few skills and little education. The only jobs open to them pay little. Their lives are poor and living conditions are worse. As the cities expand, it is harder than ever for poor people to make a living.

To add to Africa's problems, *AIDS* has hit several nations hard.

Think About It:

Destroying the ability of land to produce food for people and animals is dangerous. How is damanged land related to people moving to the cities?

Is Peace Only a Dream?

In December 1979, Rhodesia's seven-year war ended. The United Nations Security Council ended its thirteen-year *economic embargo*. Rhodesia could again trade with the rest of the world.

In March of the next year, *Robert Mugabe*, a guerrilla leader, became the first president of *Zimbabwe*. This was Rhodesia's new name.

Groups and tribes in Zimbabwe did not get along. In 1983, *Joshua Nkomo* had to flee after Mugabe ordered mass arrests of his political foes. Mugabe and Nkomo both fought against the British. When victory came, one group took total control of the new nation.

South Africa still searched for peace. Blacks demanded rights and a voice in government. Whites refused their demands.

South Africa set up black *townships* or *homelands* for black residents only. Blacks working in cities traveled to the city to work. Then they returned to a township to live.

Racial tension increased in South Africa. In 1984, riots in black townships left 14 dead. Hundreds were injured as police clashed with blacks. By July 1985, the government imposed a *state of emergency.* This took people's rights away and increased government control. In May of the next year, black workers staged the biggest strike ever seen in South Africa.

Slowly, many white South Africans agreed change had to come. Blacks were given more rights. By September 1989, the government allowed blacks to demonstrate. Soon, members of the *African National Congress* (ANC) were released from prison. In 1990, the most famous of all ANC leaders got out of prison. *Nelson Mandela* had been locked up for 27 years for opposing white government.

Nelson Mandela

Mandela and white government leaders met and talked about future plans. The police began to relax their control. By late summer, black groups were fighting each other. Members of the *Zulu* tribe fought other Africans. Within weeks over 500 Africans were killed. The army moved in to restore order.

Think About It:

South Africa is only one nation in which African tribes fought other tribes. Why did people of the same nation fight each other once the nation was free from foreign rule?

During the 1980's, *Colonel Muammar Gadhafi* of *Libya* became a leader in world terrorism. He supported terrorist groups in Northern Ireland and the Middle East. Early in 1986, the United States broke relations with Libya.

Libya was linked to several brutal terrorist attacks in Europe. As a result, U.S. warplanes bombed Gadhafi's Libyan base in April 1986.

In 1990, *Liberia* was in a state of civil war. U.S. ships and Marines were sent to evacuate Americans there.

Foreign rule is over in Africa. Age-old problems remain.

A Quick Review

Fill in each blank with the name or term that best fits.

1. What was once Rhodesia is now two countries, _____ and

   _____.

2. The European nation of _____ sent troops to help Chad fight Libya in the 1980's.

3. The rapid increase in _____ in many African nations is harming the land and causing human suffering.

4. Robert _____, a former guerrilla leader, became the first president of Zimbabwe.

5. The nation of _____ created black townships to separate blacks from whites.

6. Swarms of insects called _____ destroy millions of acres of crops in Africa during certain years.

7. A state of _____ limits human rights and gives more power to the government.

8. African National Congress leader Nelson _____ was freed after 27 years in prison.

World Knowledge Expands

With the space age came a great expansion of knowledge.

Computers did in seconds what had taken hours or even years with pencil and paper. *Artificial intelligence* was taken seriously. It seemed possible that computers could be designed to think.

Robots were developed to do jobs that were repeated over and over. They also did jobs that were dangerous for humans.

The space program advanced rapidly. In April 1981, the first space shuttle returned safely from orbit. *Columbia* landed in California. The age of reusable spacecraft had arrived.

Two years later *Sally Ride* became the first American woman in space aboard space shuttle *Challenger.*

Many advances came as a result of the space program. Special clay products called *ceramics* were designed as heat shields. They protect spacecraft when coming back through the atmosphere to earth. These same ceramic discoveries are valuable in homes and industries.

Laser beams of concentrated light are used in medicine for delicate surgery. In industry they cut massive pieces of material.

Advances in medicine came quickly. New and better *antibiotics* were discovered. Anti-rejection drugs made it possible to do successful *organ* transplants.

In December 1982, *Barney Clark* was dying of heart failure. He received the first *artificial* heart. It was called Jarvik-7 and was made of plastic and metal. Though Clark did not live long, he proved an artificial heart might be possible. Two years later a permanent artificial heart was given to William Schroeder. He lived 620 days.

But not all medical news was good. In 1981, the world first heard of *AIDS.* Acquired Immune Deficiency Syndrome has no known cure. It destroys the body's ability to fight disease. AIDS is transmitted through blood and other body fluids.

People realized the need for better mass transportation. France, Great Britain, and Japan have passenger trains that travel over 100 miles per hour.

High-speed train

As OPEC raised oil prices, nations looked for ways to conserve gas and oil. *Solar power* seemed one answer to saving fuel. Thousands of homes installed solar panels. These convert the sun's energy into power to heat water and light and heat entire homes.

Contests are held to see which college can build the best and fastest solar-powered auto. In July 1981, the first solar-powered airplane flew across the English Channel.

Think About It:

Solar power does not pollute and is never used up. Why isn't it used more to replace oil as fuel?

Many of the plans for fuel conservation ended in the mid-1980's. Due to earlier conservation and more fuel-efficient autos, the world had more oil than it needed. This petroleum *glut* caused oil prices to fall.

With cheaper gasoline and home heating fuel, many people forgot to conserve. American auto companies built larger cars and vans. These use more gasoline. Families turned their thermostats up.

Increasing fuel use caused another problem, though. *Pollution* also increased. Auto and factory emissions fouled the air. City and factory waste fouled lakes and rivers. Better waste disposal was demanded. Cleaner-burning fuels and emission controls were required.

Waste disposal sites filled up. Some things, such as aluminum and paper, are *recycled*. New technology is needed to recycle products like paper, glass, and plastic even better.

Toxic waste made the news. Many by-products from manufacturing cause disease or kill.

Emissions from vehicles and factories form harmful acids in the air. *Acid rain* was also created by utility companies. Lakes were harmed and entire forests died.

In nations such as Brazil and Indonesia the tropical *rain forest* is being destroyed. Farmers burn the forest to get land for crops. The thin soil only raises a few crops. Then the farmers destroy more forest.

The problem for the world is that trees turn carbon dioxide into oxygen. Without oxygen people and animals die. The loss of rain forests holds danger for our future.

The *ozone layer* made the news in the 1980's. This part of our atmosphere helps protect us from damaging rays from the sun. The ozone layer seems to be harmed by human-made gasses called chlorofluorocarbons (CFC's). These were used in air conditioners, refrigerators, insulation, and some spray cans.

Another threat is also related to changes in our atmosphere. As emissions collect, they form a barrier in the air. This holds heat in rather than letting it escape into space. The *greenhouse effect* is a heating of the earth by the heat that is trapped. If the earth's temperature rises only slightly, some farm areas will dry up. They will become deserts. Polar ice caps may melt. This will raise the level of the oceans.

Think About It:
Look at a world map or globe. See how many major cities are at the edge of the ocean. How many will flood if the oceans rise only a few feet?

Scientists don't know for sure if humans are causing the earth to heat up. A change in temperature may be part of a normal cycle of change.

The world was shocked when a space tragedy took place January 31, 1985. The space shuttle *Challenger* blew up during launch. Seven astronauts died. The US. space program was halted for three years.

The next year a Soviet nuclear generating plant went out of control. The plant at *Chernobyl* released deadly radiation. This was carried by the wind for hundreds of miles. Thousands of people were exposed to dangerous amounts of radiation. The land around Chernobyl is now useless. Nations in Europe found that animals that ate radioactive grass were also radioactive. They had to be destroyed. People began to understand what can happen if there is a nuclear accident.

In 1988, another problem of technology was revealed. A *computer virus* was programmed into a computer network. Thousands of scientific and government computers had to be shut down. A prank by a college student showed how much we depend on computers and how easy it is to damage the information they hold.

The 1980's ended with the launching of a huge space telescope. It cost billions of dollars. However, a flaw in the lens caused the telescope's photos to blur. Repairs were made later by the crew of a space shuttle. The repaired *Hubble* telescope gives us a look into space never before possible.

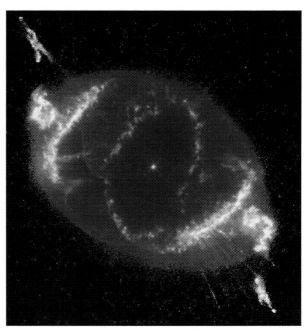

Rings of gas surround the dying star NGC 6543, nicknamed the Cat's Eye (as seen from the Hubble Telescope).

How far the world has come since the first space satellite was launched!

Think About It:
Trains, autos, electric lights, and telephones were once new technologies. Many people feared them for a time. Today, some people are afraid of space exploration, computers, and nuclear power. How do we know whether a technological advance is good or not?

Checking Up

Read each statement below. Pick the name or term from the list that best completes the statement. Write your choice in the space provided. Don't use any items from the list more than once. Some you won't use at all.

acid rain	AIDS	artificial	*Challenger*
Chernobyl	Clark	*Columbia*	glut
greenhouse	ozone	rain forests	Ride
solar	stealth	toxic	viruses

1. The first American woman astronaut was Sally _____.

2. A terrible nuclear accident in the Soviet Union took place at

   _____.

3. Something that is _____ can cause disease or death.

4. The first person to receive an artificial heart was Barney _____.

5. Destruction of the _____ layer can expose us to harmful rays from the sun.

6. The _____ effect may result in heating of the earth's surface to higher than normal temperatures.

7. The first U.S. space shuttle was named _____.

8. Commands given to computers that will destroy the computer's programs or slow them down are known as computer _____.

9. A disease that became widespread in the 1980's and that cannot be cured is called _____.

10. A computer that can think for itself would have what we call _____ intelligence.

TOWARD THE TWENTY-FIRST CENTURY

Introduction

An entire generation lived with the cold war, iron curtain, and atomic bomb. Fear of war and communism were part of daily living.

The 1980's opened with relations between the West and the Soviet Union as bad as ever. Drugs were becoming more dangerous. The Middle East was full of problems.

As the twenty-first century approached, the world had survived many changes. Small wars had been fought. The Soviet Union had ceased to exist. The nations of Europe were trying to unite their economies. What had once been Yugoslavia was now several small states where NATO soldiers tried to keep the peace.

The Middle East was still unstable. The economies of many Asian nations were a mess. India and Pakistan still hated one another. Illegal drug use seemed more serious than ever.

Danger, Drugs, and Democracy in Latin America

Mexico is a nation of rapid *population* growth and great poverty. It looked as though Mexico's *petroleum* discoveries would provide money needed to help the nation's poor. When oil prices dropped, the country's hopes faded.

Less money went to Mexico to pay for oil. The government had borrowed billions of dollars from the United States and other nations. When oil income dropped, Mexico could not repay its debts.

Millions of poor farm families moved to Mexico City and other cities hoping for a better life. They found slums and no jobs. Other millions of poor Mexicans caused problems by entering the United States illegally.

Some Mexican citizens became part of the illegal *drug trade. Cocaine* grown and refined in *Colombia* comes to Mexico. From there it is smuggled into the United States.

The United States and Mexico cooperate in many ways. In 1993, Mexico, Canada, and the United States signed the North American Free Trade Agreement. *NAFTA* means that Canada, the U.S., and Mexico can trade with one another more easily. NAFTA means more jobs for workers in Mexico. It also means better markets for Mexico's products.

But NAFTA did not help the poor farmers in much of Mexico. Rebels in *Chiapas* province began to attack government forces. The government struck back. Soldiers died. So did poor farmers. The farmers demanded better conditions. The government says it is trying.

By the end of 1994, the Mexican *peso* dropped in value. The next January the United States began to loan Mexico huge amounts of money. Otherwise, Mexico faced a financial crisis. The good news is that Mexico was able to repay the loans.

Bad news came when Mexico's drug czar was linked to the drug cartel. Evidence followed that some Mexican officials and banks were deeply involved in the drug trade.

Further south in some Central American nations, danger and death were everywhere. The 1980's became the turning point in a long struggle for power. For many years, right-wing dictators had allowed power and wealth to belong to very few people in their countries. Because these dictators were not communists, the United States often backed them. Sometimes the U.S. backed them even when it did not approve of everything they did.

When poor people saw the U.S. support for these dictators, some of them turned to the Soviet Union and Cuba for help when they tried to overthrow their governments. Sometimes they were successful in their revolutions, like in *Nicaragua*. Sometimes they were not, like in *El Salvador*. But in all cases the wars brought death and terror. Right-wing death squads and left-wing guerrillas both killed many people.

Fortunately, during the 1990's, the worst acts of both sides seemed to be ending. A balance was being found to allow everyone a fairer chance to create a good life. In 1996, even the 36-year-old civil war in *Guatemala* finally ended.

Think About It:

The United States government gave aid to those in Central America who opposed Communism. Should the U.S. have had any say in what sort of government these small nations chose?

The nation of *Panama* is important because of the *Panama Canal*. The U.S. agreed to give Panama more control over the canal. By the end of the century Panama will own the canal.

Panama Canal

However, Panama was ruled by a powerful military dictator, *Manuel Noriega*. He made money from helping drug dealers. He controlled the army. The people of Panama could do nothing against Noriega. In 1990, the United States invaded Panama and captured Noriega.

Earlier, Cuba sent Communist workers to the island of *Grenada* in the Caribbean. These workers were building an air base. In 1983, U.S. troops invaded the tiny island. They captured hundreds of Cuban engineers, workers, and soldiers. This did not help Cuba's relations with the United States.

For 28 years the U.S. accepted refugees from Cuba. During President Clinton's term in office, this policy changed several times.

In 1996 Cuba's relations with the U.S. hit another snag. Cuban military jets shot down two small civilian airplanes from Florida. However, by 1998 the two nations seemed less angry with each other.

The small island nation of *Haiti* is also in the Caribbean Sea. Its people are poor and have suffered from corrupt governments. Things got so bad that in 1991 the United States cut off aid to Haiti.

The United Nations began trying to restore democracy to Haiti. Finally, after a trade embargo and a United Nations threat to invade, things changed.

The military officals gave up their government offices in September 1994. About 5000 troops from the U.S. landed to supervise the government. The next year United Nations troops replaced the U.S. soldiers in Haiti. In December the people of Haiti elected a new president.

In South America several nations struggled, including **Brazil**. Brazil is huge and has many natural resources. But many Brazilians are poor. Brazil owes huge amounts of money to the United States and other nations. And in the mid-1990's the president of Brazil resigned when he faced charges of corruption.

Next door to Brazil is **Venezuela**. That nation's president was also tried for graft in 1993.

At the other end of South America, the military ruled **Argentina**. In 1982, Argentina invaded the **Falkland Islands** in the Atlantic Ocean. Great Britain had claimed the islands for 149 years and went to war when Argentina invaded. After a short war Argentina surrendered.

The next year military rule ended in Argentina. The new president put military leaders on trial for their terrorist activities.

Argentina suffered from problems of inflation and lack of ability to produce enough goods to pay for all its people's needs.

Peru and Chile had their own troubles, but none were so bad as those of **Colombia**. Colombia was the cocaine-exporting capital of the world. **Drug dealers** had their own private armies and were above government control.

The government tried to control the drug trade. Judges and police were terrorized and killed. Drug dealers planted bombs in cities such as **Bogotá**. Thousands died, including newspaper publishers and reporters.

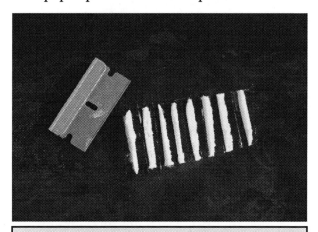

Think About It:

Poverty is a part of life for millions in South America. Colombia's poor farmers raise coca, which becomes cocaine. How can these farmers be persuaded to raise other crops that pay them much less than coca?

Good Things and Bad in Asia

Once the war in Vietnam ended, the Communist government controlled all of that nation. By 1979, Vietnamese troops took control of the nation of **Cambodia**. That same year Vietnam and China fought a small border war that neither side won.

In 1990, the Vietnamese began withdrawing from Cambodia. In the following years the United States began giving financial aid to Vietnam. In return Vietnam helped the U.S. search for troops still missing from the war.

The United States ended its trade embargo with Vietnam in 1994. The next year the two nations exchanged diplomats. U.S. tourists and businesses became common in

Vietnam. The two enemy nations seemed to put the war behind them.

Soviet troops had moved into *Afghanistan* in 1979. The Marxist government there needed help to stay in power.

The Soviets could not defeat the rebel fighters in the mountains of Afghanistan. The war ended for the Soviets the way the war in Vietnam ended for the United States. After ten years of fighting, the Soviet army had to withdraw. In April 1992, guerrillas from six rebel groups met in the capital city. They declared that Afghanistan was now an Islamic republic.

This did not bring peace to Afghanistan. *Taliban* guerrillas fought other forces. In 1996, the Taliban forces took control of the nation's capital.

As the century ended, the Talibans ruled most of Afghanistan. Women have almost no rights. Citizens are punished or killed for doing anything the Taliban leaders do not approve of. Most other Islamic nations do not approve of what has happened in Afghanistan.

In another part of Asia, in 1983, *Benigno Aquino* was running for president of the *Philippines.* He was assassinated in the city of Manila. His widow, *Corazon*, was elected president. The former president, Ferdinand Marcos, and his wife had to leave the Philippines.

India and *Pakistan* continued to have problems. In 1991, India's former prime minister was assassinated. *Rajiv Gandhi* was running for re-election when he was killed. India's unstable government fell again in April 1997.

In Pakistan, Mrs. *Benazir Bhutto* was elected prime minister in 1993. The army had helped force her out of office three years before. Then, in 1996, she was out of office

once again. In February 1997, Pakistan elected a Muslim government.

Neither Pakistan nor India had governments that stayed in power very long. Each new government tried to show it was strong. This was partly to blame for what happened in the spring of 1998. Both nations had argued and fought over the land known as *Kashmir.* Kashmir is on the border between India and Pakistan.

China sent new weapons to Pakistan. India said it would begin testing its nuclear weapons. U.S. President Clinton asked India not to do this. India went ahead with a number of underground nuclear tests.

Pakistan said it would also test its nuclear weapons. Again Clinton asked for restraint. Pakistan exploded several underground weapons.

Two more nations now had nuclear weapons.

China was a major newsmaker as the century drew toward a close. This huge nation tried to slow its population growth. The Communist government had total power. The birth rate did slow down.

In the early 1980's, China began to change toward capitalism. The Chinese leader Deng Xiaoping was a practical man. He opened China to Western technology and management styles. U.S. President Reagan visited China in the spring of 1984. His influence helped Deng to keep the changes going.

The Chinese people also hoped for less government control. In April 1989, Chinese students began a protest in *Beijing.* They gathered in the city center, called *Tiananmen Square.* They called for democracy. Workers cheered the students and began to demand more freedom. By May over a million students and workers were in the streets. On June 9 and 10, the government cracked down. The military moved in. Executions began. The student protest was crushed.

China agreed to the Nuclear Non-Proliferation Treaty in 1991. It was the last major nation to agree to stop the spread of atomic weapons. But it didn't stop its own weapons program. Two years later China set off an underground nuclear explosion. It set off another in 1996.

China made little progress in human rights. It also continued to threaten Taiwan. In spite of this, the U.S. gave China favored trade status in 1994 and 1996. President Clinton said China was too big a nation to isolate. And some American businesses were beginning to do well in China.

But there were still problems. In the *Information Age*, it's easy for people to use computers to steal things. The Chinese had been doing just that. In 1995, China and the U.S. reached an agreement on copyright. China said it would stop stealing copyrighted books and other products. And in 1996, China agreed to help stop property piracy. The Chinese said they would stop stealing U.S. product designs.

Great Britain turned Hong Kong over to China in July 1997. This increased China's economic strength. It also meant the people of Hong Kong may have less freedom at least for now than they had in the past.

During the 1980's *Japan* led the world in manufacturing and finance. It became the leading economic nation in the world. Japan controlled many of the world's largest banks. It had a high standard of living. Japanese products were shipped all over the world. Since the Japanese did not have a costly military, their nation prospered.

Think About It:

The United States promised to protect Japan in case of war. Japan was able to spend money to improve its economy instead of paying for a military force. How did this have a major effect on the U.S. economy?

In the following years Japan's economy slowed. For the first time ever, Japanese workers were laid off. Banks and financial companies failed. Some leaders killed themselves in shame.

In 1995, Japan faced a different problem. Japanese terrorists struck in *Tokyo*. Nerve gas was released in the subways by a religious cult. A dozen people died and five thousand were injured.

Other nations in southeast Asia, such as Indonesia, had the same economic troubles as Japan. Rulers were not completely honest in some cases. In others the leaders felt good economic conditions would last forever.

As the twentieth century neared an end, Japan and many of its neighbors were having great economic problems. *South Korea* had been as successful as Japan. Some of its biggest companies were now in trouble. A few were nearly broke.

South Korea and *North Korea* did begin to talk about getting along better. However, North Korea withdrew from the nuclear treaty in 1993. By the end of the year, North Korea refused to allow inspection of their nuclear plants.

Meanwhile North Korea was in the midst of a famine. Its people needed food. Other nations helped supply food.

North Korea began a new nuclear policy. They agreed not to build atomic weapons.

The final two years of the century were not calm in Asia.

Economic problems continued. Japan tried several ways of improving the nation's economy. None of them worked very well. For the first time in fifty years people lost their jobs. The value of stocks dropped. The world's second largest economy was in big trouble.

Malaysia and other nations in Southeast Asia were suffering as well. Jobs were lost. People had no confidence in their governments. Perhaps worst off was *Indonesia.* By early 1999 twenty million people were out of work in Indonesia.

In some nations, such as Indonesia, religious groups fought each other. There was a good chance civil war might break out.

Russia's economy was a disaster. The value of Russian money dropped. Criminals took control of many cities. Foreign investors were afraid to invest more money in Russia. The nation could not repay loans from other countries. Many Russians wanted to return to Communism.

Afghanistan remained a problem nation. A rich terrorist named *Bin Laden* set up a training camp in Afghanistan. He was probably responsible when two United States embassies were bombed in Africa.

President Clinton ordered missile strikes on Bin Laden's camp in Afghanistan. He also had a chemical factory in Sudan attacked. Bin Laden was not hurt in the attack. He vowed to attack more U.S. sites and citizens. On the bright side, Afghanistan leaders claimed he left their country in early 1999.

North Korea entered the twenty-first century as an unsolved problem. That nation had already tested a long-range missile. It seemed likely North Korea was still working on nuclear weapons.

Africa in the Balance

In 1990, *Nelson Mandela* headed the African National Congress. Later, the government and the African National Congress met and talked about the future of *South Africa.* By the end of the year, racial discrimination in public places was illegal.

Schools in South Africa were integrated in January 1991. Change was truly happening.

In 1994, Nelson Mandela ran for president. He was elected in the first election in South Africa in which everyone could vote. South Africa had a black president.

Soon other nations began to trade with South Africa again. Conflicts still exist in government and in daily life. But democratic rights are improving for most of the nation's black citizens.

In *Ethiopia* a Marxist dictator ruled for seventeen years. In 1991, he resigned and left the country. Rebels were advancing on the capital. The United States was asked to arrange a settlement. In 1993, the province of Eritrea won freedom from Ethiopia after years of fighting.

At the same time U.S.-backed rebels in *Angola* agreed with the Marxist government to hold free elections. The 16-year-old war ended in June. Another African nation prepared for democracy. However, it wasn't until 1994 that a formal peace treaty was signed with the rebels. The next year the UN had to send peacekeepers to Angola.

To the north of Angola the nation of *Libya* kept on causing trouble. In 1984, a gunman in the Libyan embassy in *London* shot and killed a female police officer. The guilty

Wreckage from
Lockerbie explosion

Libyan left England without being punished.
He was a diplomat.

In 1988, a Pan Am 747 jet exploded over
Lockerbie, Scotland. A bomb went off in the
cargo area. All 259 people aboard the plane
died. So did 11 who were on the ground. Two
Libyan men were accused of the bombing.
Libya refused to turn them over for trial. In
1992 the United Nations imposed sanctions
on Libya. Air travel and arms sales were
stopped until the two were turned over for
trial. Negotiations were underway for where
to hold their trial as the century ended.

For most of recent history another African nation has also been struggling with a
civil war—*Sudan.* As late as 1998 the people
of one part of Sudan were buying and selling
other Sudanese as slaves.

On the east side of Africa, people in
Somalia were starving. The United Nations
vowed to protect food supplies. Warlords
from different clans were taking the food
donated to help the starving.

In December 1992, U.S. troops entered
Somalia. Their job was to make sure food
supplies were kept away from the warlords.
Even though U.S. troops were present, fighting between the clans continued. Riots broke
out.

Troops in Somalia

A larger UN peacekeeping force arrived.
The United States turned over control of the
peacekeeping to the UN. By the middle of
1993, U.S. and UN troops attacked one of the
Somali warlords. But nothing the U.S. or the
UN could do seemed to help. U.S. troops
pulled out by the end of March 1994. A year
later, the last of the UN troops left as well.
The warlords were still in power. People still
needed help. It seemed that short of war, the
UN could not change things in Somalia.

Things were no better in the center of Africa. In April 1994, a plane crash killed the presidents of **Burundi** and **Rwanda**. Almost at once fighting broke out between the Tutsi and Hutu tribes in Rwanda. In a short time 200,000 people died in Rwanda. Another 250,000 escaped to Tanzania.

The civil war continued into May. The UN sent in African troops as peacekeepers. They arrived too late to save the lives of half a million people who died in the fighting.

By the middle of the summer, the rebels claimed victory. The UN investigated acts of genocide. One tribe deliberately tried to kill everyone of the other tribe. By then 2,000,000 people from Rwanda had fled into Zaire.

Once the fighting stopped, refugees slowly returned. By the end of 1996 half a million people had come back to Rwanda.

Zaire had not been safe for the refugees. Beginning in 1993, rebels started to fight government troops. By 1997, the rebels were demanding the government's overthrow. They advanced toward the nation's capital. In May they took over Zaire and set up a new government.

In 1995, the president of **Algeria** was re-elected. This followed a civil war with Islamic fundamentalists. As many as 40,000 people were killed in Algeria's civil conflict. During 1997 and 1998 more villagers were murdered.

In 1996, foreigners had to flee **Liberia**. Once again the citizens of that nation were fighting each other.

Think About It:

In many ways things improved in Africa during the final years of the twentieth century. In other areas things were as bad as ever. What will it take to bring an end to civil wars in some African nations?

Africa ended the twentieth century with unsolved problems.

South Africa's government was not able to keep all its promises. Members of different tribes fought one another.

In Ethiopia, troops along the border fought for barren lands.

Members of one tribe still hated those from other tribes in central Africa. Several times American and European visitors were attacked and killed in Kenya.

Terrorists in Libya remained safe. Two airline bombers were to be tried by a court in the Netherlands. They stayed in Libya. Six terrorists were tried in France even though they were still in Libya.

The Cold War Is Over

Soviet leader **Mikhail Gorbachev** knew change was coming. When he took over the U.S.S.R. in 1985, he called for economic development. He and U.S. President Reagan met in Geneva for conferences. For the first time in 40 years, there was a chance the cold war might end.

In 1988, Reagan flew to **Moscow** for a summit conference with Gorbachev. The Russian people welcomed Reagan. Gorbachev told his people change was necessary.

On Nobember 9, 1989, the first holes were made in the **Berlin Wall**. The **iron curtain** was coming down. The cold war seemed at an end.

The Berlin Wall coming down

In the Soviet Union the Communists gave up much of their power. Gorbachev planned to form a Western style government.

By March 1990, the Communists had lost political control of several major Soviet cities. Two months later citizens in **Estonia** and **Latvia** demonstrated. They wanted to be free of Soviet rule. Their neighbor, **Lithuania**, began talks with Gorbachev about freedom for that nation. A little over a year later, in August 1991, these three nations got their wish. For the first time since World War II, Latvia, Estonia, and Lithuania were free!

In May 1990, **Boris Yeltsin** was elected president of Russia, the largest nation in the Soviet Union. The next month Gorbachev met with U.S. President Bush in Washington, D.C. They talked about limiting chemical and nuclear weapons.

By October the U.S. and the Soviets agreed on a new arms pact. The Soviets said they would destroy thousands of tanks and big guns based in Europe.

In the summer of 1991, the U.S. and the Soviet Union signed a Strategic Arms agreement. Talks had gone on for nine years. Both nations would cut back on their long-range missiles. The United States and other Western nations promised to help the Soviet Union as it changed from Communism.

In December 1991, the Soviet Union ceased to exist. Russia and 10 other former Soviet republics joined to form the Commonwealth of Independent States. Change was difficult. Shops were still bare. Wages were poor. People began to protest. Now that the Communists were not in control, protest was possible.

In 1992, the seven major industrial nations gave the Commonwealth a one-year aid program. It amounted to $24 billion. Without it the new government would collapse.

In 1994, NATO talked about admitting some nations that had been under Soviet control. That summer *Russia* joined NATO as a "partner." As a partner Russia could take part in some NATO military exercises and peacekeeping jobs.

Some parts of the old Soviet Union were still under Russia's control. In March 1995, the region of *Chechnya* demanded independence. Its Muslim citizens hated Russian rule. Russian troops invaded Chechnya. The Russians were able to advance slowly.

The Russian army captured cities and land in Chechnya. To everyone's surprise the rebels slowed the Russian troops. They even attacked a town in Russia.

The fighting in Chechnya went on for months. The fact that the tiny rebel army was able to hold its own against the Russians was important. Eventually a truce was called. Chechnya remained under Russian control. But the army the world had feared was no longer the power it had once been.

NATO agreed to cut back its troops in Europe. So did Russia. The Russian economy was so bad that Russia did not want to spend money on an army in Europe.

Think About It:

Communist governments controlled workers, farms, and manufacturing. When these controls ended with the Soviet Union, conditions did not improve. What are some possible reasons the Russian economy actually got worse as people had more freedom?

Compare Turn-of-the-Century Europe with Post-War Europe

Compare this map with the Post-War Europe map on page 127. Use both maps to answer these questions.

1. What changes took place in East and West Germany?

   _____

   _____

   _____

2. What national changes occurred on Poland's southern border?

   _____

   _____

   _____

3. New nations emerged from the land once controlled by the Soviet Union. Name three of these new nations.

   _____

   _____

   _____

4. What was once Yugoslavia was divided into new nations. Name the five nations formed from Yugoslavia that are shown on the map.

   _____

   _____

   _____

   _____

Gorbachev was right when he told his people change was coming. As early as 1980, shipyard workers in **Poland** went on strike. NATO warned the Soviet Union to stay out of Poland. **Detente** was cooperation between the West and the Soviet Union. It would not survive if the Soviets invaded Poland.

The Polish government crushed that strike and others. Labor leader **Lech Walesa** was put in jail. Polish police broke up **Solidarity** rallies. The government outlawed that labor union.

Solidarity rally

Walesa got out of jail. In 1983, the Polish government ended its military law. Lech Walesa got the ***Nobel Peace Prize.*** Six years later Poland decided to hold free and open elections.

About the same time, ***Václav Havel***, who opposed the Communists, was released from prison in ***Czechoslovakia.*** Soon afterwards, he was elected president of that nation. In 1993 Czechoslovakia became two nations. They were the ***Czech Republic*** and ***Slovakia.***

During the summer of 1990, 24 industrial nations promised help to nations of Eastern Europe. These nations had been controlled by the Soviet Union for many years. They included Czechoslovakia, Bulgaria, Yugoslavia, East Germany, Poland, and Hungary. Seven years later the Czech Republic, Hungary, and Poland were invited to join NATO.

Big changes came for ***East Germany*** once Soviet rule ended. In October 1990, East and West Germany were united. The last Soviet troops were withdrawn. For the first time in decades, citizens were free to travel from East to West Germany. The first free elections since 1933 were held in East Germany.

Now it was up to West Germany to do something about East Germany's terrible economy. This was hard to do. West Germans had to pay extra taxes to help the Eastern part of the united nation. East German factories were out of date. The people knew little about working in modern plants. Unemployment was high.

East Germany's poor economy pulled down the rich western part of the nation. Beginning in 1992, neo-Nazis began to demonstrate and cause trouble. They said they wanted Germany for Germans. They blamed the lack of jobs on immigrants.

As the century closed, the former East Germany was still not prosperous. The entire Germany economy suffered from unification.

The neo-Nazi party seemed stronger than ever. Other nations in Eastern Europe struggled to learn how to live without Communism.

In 1989, the Communist party in Hungary became the Socialist party. Communist leaders in ***Rumania*** and ***Bulgaria*** were overthrown.

The small nation of ***Albania*** was quick to work toward democracy. Not much was heard about its success until 1997. In the spring a huge investment plan collapsed. Citizens had invested in what they thought was a sure thing. It was a fraud. Thousands of people lost their life savings. Riots broke out.

By summer Albania had a new government. Its people had learned a terrible lesson: Freedom requires you to watch out for yourself. Harm can come from many directions.

Yugoslavia was a nation formed from several smaller regions after World War I. Under the Communist leadership of President Tito, it was a stable country. So, no one was prepared for what happened when Communist rule ended in Yugoslavia. The several smaller regions suddenly began to fight among themselves.

The biggest country has kept the name ***Yugoslavia*** and is made up of ***Serbia*** and Montenegro. The other countries are ***Slovenia***, ***Macedonia***, ***Croatia***, and ***Bosnia and Herzegovina***. Although the last country really does have a double name, it will be called Bosnia from here on.

Two of the countries, Slovenia and Macedonia, managed to get autonomy, or self-rule, with very little or no fighting. They became nations in 1992. However, the Serbs in Yugoslavia didn't want to let the rest of the country go. Croats had to fight a little harder to get their own country. But Croatia, too, became a nation in 1992.

Bosnia was not so lucky. Three ethnic groups live in Bosnia. Each ethnic group has its own background and culture. Bosnian Serbs were happy to help the Yugoslavs fight in their land. Bosnian Croats and Muslims formed an alliance to fight the Serbs.

From 1992 until 1996, Bosnia suffered a bloodbath. The Serbs laid siege to Sarajevo, the capital city of Bosnia. They tried to starve and freeze out anyone they couldn't kill by military means. Countless Muslim lives were lost. All over Bosnia, the Serbs drove Muslims from their homes in a campaign of *ethnic cleansing*. Many of the Muslims were later found in mass graves. By the end of the fighting, at least 24,000 Muslims were missing. Serbs were trying to do to the Bosnian Muslims what Hitler had done to the Jews during World War II.

Finally, in 1996, the fighting stopped. Bosnia was divided into parts—the Bosnian Serb Republic and the Muslim-Croat federation. The UN and the U.S. provided peacekeeping troops to make sure the peace was kept. War crimes trials began in the Netherlands. And for a while, Bosnia was out of the news.

In spite of peace agreements, Serbia was not peaceful. The Serbs invaded the Yugoslavian province of *Kosovo*. Most of the people living in Kosovo were Albanians.

NATO intervened to stop the ethnic cleansing. NATO forces dropped bombs on Yugoslavia. The Serbs agreed to leave Kosovo.

One thing was certain. The nation that was once *Yugoslavia* was not a peaceful place. People of one group hated people from another group. The only way to keep them from killing one another was for U.S. and NATO troops to remain on guard. It seemed a problem with no solution.

Think About It:

Ethnic and religious hatreds seem to be behind much of the fighting at the turn of the century—in the Middle East, in the former Yugoslavia, in Africa. Can you think of any ways to solve this sort of problem, so international peacekeepers will no longer be needed?

Margaret Thatcher (1925–   )

Margaret Thatcher was the first woman prime minister of Great Britain. When she took office, the nation was a comprehensive welfare state. Major industries were owned by the government. Labor unions were very strong, and Great Britain's economy was weak. Mrs. Thatcher changed much of that.

She was born in Grantham, England, on October 13, 1925. She and her sister grew up in a home without indoor plumbing or hot water. Her father, who was in politics, encouraged Margaret to get involved in politics too.

After earning a chemistry degree from Oxford University, she married Denis Thatcher in 1951. In 1953, Margaret gave birth to twins, Carol and Mark. She also passed her bar exam to become a barrister (lawyer).

Margaret Thatcher worked in politics. In 1975 she became the first woman to lead the Conservative party. She talked to the British people about her ideas for the economy. Many people were tired of the powerful unions. In 1979, it seemed everyone was on strike. Strikes by garbage collectors, hospital workers, and teachers made people angry. They voted Mrs. Thatcher into power. In May 1979, she became prime minister.

As prime minister, Mrs. Thatcher made major changes. She cut taxes on earnings, which made people happy. Industries that didn't perform well were sold to become private businesses. However, unemployment rose and her unpopularity rose too. She was nicknamed The Iron Lady.

In April 1982, Argentina attacked the British-controlled Falkland Islands. The government put down the attack in ten weeks. Mrs. Thatcher's popularity rose.

In June 1983, Mrs. Thatcher was re-elected as prime minister. During this term many British people became stockholders in industries the government used to own. Inflation dropped and the amount of money people could spend rose. Union membership fell by 25 percent. The unions were not as powerful as they had been.

In 1987, Mrs. Thatcher was the first prime minister in 160 years to be elected to a third consecutive term. After her popularity declined, she resigned as prime minister in November, 1990.

In 1979, an IRA bomb killed Earl ***Mountbatten*** of Great Britain. He was one of many to die as a result of problems in ***Northern Ireland.***

The London Stock Exchange was bombed the following summer. Citizens of Northern Ireland died, as well as a member of Parliament.

In February 1991, the IRA fired at the home of the prime minister. The same month, bombs exploded in two of London's biggest railway stations. More bombs exploded in London.

The prime ministers of Great Britain and Ireland proposed a peace plan the next year.

Peace seemed possible when a cease-fire was called by the IRA in August 1994. The killing by the IRA and Protestant extremists had gone on for 25 years. By the end of the year, British and Sinn Fein leaders met to discuss peace.

A little more than a year later, the IRA broke the cease-fire. The killing began again.

However, by the summer of 1997 another cease-fire began. British prime minister Tony Blair met with leaders of both sides in Northern Ireland. George Mitchell, a former U.S. Senate Majority Leader, helped the two sides work out their problems.

In May 1998, a vote was taken in Northern Ireland. People voted for peace. There were still shootings and bombings. It was too early to tell whether the vote for peace would overcome years of hatred.

Not all of Europe was fighting. Most of the nations were working toward becoming a united Europe. This was an outgrowth of the Common Market. In November 1993, Germany became the twelfth nation to sign the European Union treaty. It was signed at ***Maastricht*** and became known as the Maastricht Treaty.

This agreement meant those nations that became part of the European Union would cooperate. They would trade freely. People could travel from one nation to another easily. All member nations would have one form of money. Perhaps most important, rules made by the European Parliament, which met in Belgium, would be followed by all members.

The plan is for the ***Euro*** to become common currency no later than 2002. By then, all nations involved will stop printing their own money.

This is one of the reasons the United Kingdom hesitated about joining the European Union. Another reason the United Kingdom waited to join is that the European Union will have the power to set tax rates for each member nation. The Union will also establish interest rates. This takes much control of the economy away from individual nations.

In 1999 the Euro was accepted by 11 nations. It was used for foreign trade during its first years. This was a major step in creating a United States of Europe.

Tony Blair was Great Britain's new prime minister. He promised the people of Great Britain they could vote on the Euro. In 1999 he said his nation would accept the Euro. Great Britain would join the European Union. There would be no vote. Over half of his people were not pleased. Only time will tell what happens.

As Europe faced the twenty-first century, some nations were ready to fight each other. Other nations seemed willing to form a new union. Europe had changed greatly in recent years. Who knew what changes might lie ahead?

Looking Back

Below are fifteen statements about events and people in Latin America, Asia, and Europe. Decide where each event took place or where each person lived or lives. In the space before each item, write an *L* if it refers to Latin America, and *A* for things in Asia, and an *E* for those in Europe.

_____   1. Guatemala's civil war ended in 1996.

_____   2. Panama is getting full control of the Panama canal.

_____   3. Palestinian terrorists attacked airports in Rome and Vienna.

_____   4. Labor leader Lech Walesa was released after eleven months in jail.

_____   5. A revolutionary government took control of Nicaragua.

_____   6. Cambodia was invaded by troops from Vietnam.

_____   7. Václav Havel was released from prison and elected to lead his nation.

_____   8. Drug lords attacked government troops and civilians in Bogotá.

_____   9. Both Indira aand Rajiv Gandhi were assassinated.

_____   10. Corazon Aquino became president and Marcos left the country.

_____   11. A Pan Am jet exploded above the town of Lockerbie, killing a total of 270 people.

_____   12. A student protest in Tiananmen Square was crushed.

_____   13. Mikhail Gorbachev agreed to cut down on the number of Soviet troops stationed in various nations.

_____   14. Indonesia suffered from unemployment and religious unrest.

_____   15. A new currency, the Euro, was introduced.

_____   16. Yugoslavia was separated into several new countries.

The Mideast Remains a World Trouble Spot

In January 1979, the *Shah of Iran* fled that nation. A month later the *Ayatollah Khomeini* returned from exile. In Iran the *Islamic* Revolution began.

On November 4, 1979, Iranian students seized the U.S. embassy. They took the Americans there as *hostages*. Two weeks later they freed the black males and most of the women. In April a hostage rescue attempt failed. The Iranians kept 52 embassy workers prisoner for 444 days.

In 1980 Iraq attacked Iran and bombed oil refineries. A long and bloody war began. Before it ended in 1989, a million people would die.

Israel sent warplanes to destroy Iraq's nuclear reactor in June 1981. Israel said it was necessary to keep Iraq from making atomic bombs.

In March 1979, Egypt's President *Anwar Sadat* and Israel's prime minister *Menachem Begin* signed a peace treaty. It was called the *Camp David Accords*. American President *Jimmy Carter* sponsored the peace talks at Camp David.

Other Arab nations turned against Egypt for making peace with Israel. In October 1981, soldiers murdered President Sadat. Vice President *Hosni Mubarak* took over as leader.

The next month a major Israeli force invaded southern *Lebanon*. They fought *Palestinian* and *Syrian* troops. Soldiers from Israel reached the city of *Beirut*. By August, *Palestine Liberation Organization (PLO)* forces began to leave Beirut. A short time later, U.S. Marines joined French and Italian troops in Beirut. They formed a peacekeeping force.

In April 1983 the U.S. embassy in Beirut was bombed by *Muslim* terrorists. In October, a truck loaded with explosives drove onto a U.S. Marine post in Beirut and killed 241 people. At the French peacekeeping headquarters, 58 people were killed in the same way. Throughout the 1980's terrorism made life dangerous in Beirut. Bombings, hijackings, and kidnapping kept happening.

> **Think About It:**
> Peacekeeping forces in Beirut tried to stop fighting to save lives. What did terrorists hope to gain by killing the peacekeepers?

In Beirut terrorist groups supported by Iran began kidnapping Americans and other Westerners. These people were held as hostages. Some were killed.

In the U.S. some people in the White House came up with a plan. Weapons were sold to Iran in exchange for the release of a few hostages. The arms money from Iran was used to supply the contra rebels in Nicaragua. The contras were rebelling against their communist government. Only two big things were wrong with this plan. The U.S. had a policy of not bargaining with terrorists. And the U.S. Congress had passed a law saying no more military aid should be sent to the contras.

> **Think About It:**
> This plan came to be called the *Iran-Contra affair*. Iran paid for arms and released hostages. Do you think it was right for the White House to get into trouble for getting some hostages released in this way? Why or why not?

Iran began to attack oil tankers in the *Persian Gulf* in 1984. British and U.S. warships entered the Gulf.

In May 1987, an Iraqi warplane attacked the *U.S.S. Stark* in the Persian Gulf. Thirty-seven Americans died.

A U.S. ship in the Gulf shot down an Iranian airliner by mistake in July 1988.

The Ayatollah Khomeini died in 1989 in Iran. But Iran's government remained very strict. Women have few rights. Western culture is not welcome. However, in 1997, a more moderate president was elected in Iran. Small changes began to appear.

In Iraq *Saddam Hussein* needed money. His war with Iran had been expensive. He demanded that *Kuwait* share its oil income with Iraq. The Kuwaiti leaders refused. Hussein threatened to invade Kuwait.

President Mubarak of Egypt met with Saddam Hussein. He promised not to invade Kuwait. A few days later, on August 2, 1990, Iraq's army rolled into Kuwait. *Saudi Arabia* was certain Iraq would attack them in a few days.

The Iraqi army in Kuwait dug in. Arab nations asked Saddam Hussein to withdraw. He refused. The UN ordered a trade embargo of Iraq. Oil pipelines leading out of Iraq were shut down. Warships from the United States, Great Britain, France, and other nations imposed a blockade. Few supplies could enter Iraq.

Saddam Hussein seized thousands of U.S. and European citizens in Kuwait and Iraq. They became human shields to protect Iraq from attack. He used some of his own people in the same way. Eventually Saddam Hussein did release his hostages.

By September the U.S. had sent airplanes to several Arab nations. The Soviet Union, which usually backed Iraq, asked Saddam Hussein to leave Kuwait. Again he refused.

U.S. warships kept Iraqi oil tankers from leaving the Gulf. U.S. President *Bush* organized a coalition to fight Iraq. Western troops began to arrive in Saudi Arabia. Forces from the Arab nations of Syria and Egypt joined the Western forces.

On January 16, 1991, a massive bombing campaign began. Airplanes attacked military targets in Kuwait and Iraq. Iraq fired Scud missiles at Israel and Saudi Arabia. Iraq dumped millions of gallons of Kuwaiti oil into the Persian Gulf. Saddam Hussein wanted to destroy water purification plants.

In February, warships pounded targets in Iraq. The Soviets tried to arrange for Iraq to leave Kuwait. The plan failed.

On February 24, the ground war began. Coalition forces drove from Saudi Arabia into Kuwait. Iraq forces retreated. They left Kuwait City in ruins. As the Iraq army retreated, Kuwait's oil wells were set on fire.

Kuwaiti oil well on fire

Coalition troops pushed into Iraq but did not go as far as the capital city. By February 27, the fighting was over. Kuwait was free. President Bush said allied forces were not to destroy Iraq.

Think About It:

U.S. President Bush persuaded many nations to join the coalition against Iraq. Why did Arab nations agree to have Western nations attack Iraq, which is an Arab country?

The U.N. ordered Saddam Hussein to pay billions of dollars for damage to Kuwait. Iraq was also told to destroy all its chemical and biological weapons.

Even as Kuwait was freed, Iraqi troops attacked *Kurdish* civilians living in Iraq. These people fled into Iran and Turkey.

By June the UN realized Saddam Hussein had lied about Iraq's nuclear weapons. When UN inspectors tried to check these weapons, Iraqi soldiers fired over their heads.

Two months later the U.S. allowed Iraq to sell oil. The money was to be used for food and medical supplies. During the following years, the people of Iraq suffered from lack of food and medicines. Most of the money from the oil went to built huge palaces for Saddam Hussein. Some may have gone to build more weapons.

In October, UN inspectors found top-secret papers in Iraq. These told of a nuclear weapons center hidden in the desert. It was not badly damaged during the war.

This began a series of problems with Iraq which dragged on for years. UN inspectors hunted for evidence of nuclear, chemical, and biological weapons. Iraq would allow inspections for a short time. Then they would block the inspectors.

The U.S., France, and Britain used warplanes to patrol the northern and southern borders of Iraq. This was to protect Shiite Muslims and Kurds living there. Saddam Hussein hated these people. The Allied warplanes were to keep Iraq's planes out of these areas.

In January 1993, Allied warplanes attacked Iraqi missile batteries. A few months later they bombed Iraqi antiaircraft guns. Saddam Hussein kept testing to see how far he could go.

All through the 1990's, Saddam Hussein kept on testing the UN. UN inspectors were not allowed to check sites. Inspectors were threatened. At times they were ordered out of Iraq.

Hussein kept on creating problems for weapons inspectors. Time after time they were kept from doing their work. Finally on December 16, 1998, U.S. and British planes attacked military targets. The attack on Iraq lasted four days. It solved nothing.

Weapon inspections ended. Airplanes from the U.S. and Great Britain patrolled the no-fly zones in north and south Iraq. Iraq began firing at these planes. The planes fired back at radar and missile sites.

It looked as though this was one more problem that would continue into the new century.

Think About It:

President Bush organized a massive coalition to oppose Iraq. Eight years later, President Clinton was able to get only Great Britain to help the U.S. What had changed?

The Mideast remained a dangerous area. In June 1995, an attempt to kill President Mubarak of Egypt failed. One year later a terrorist bomb killed 19 U.S. troops in Saudi Arabia.

Iran bought military weapons from Russia and China.

In March 1988, the Palestinians living in Israel began an uprising. Outside nations financed the uprising which went on for years. Hundreds were killed.

Muslim guerrilla forces were firing rockets into Israel from southern Lebanon. In February 1992, Israeli helicopters and artillery struck back.

That summer in a peace bid Israel agreed to stop building homes for Jewish settlers in the West Bank and Gaza Strip.

The following summer Israel troops killed 130 people in a raid into Lebanon. Closer to home, Israel and Palestine were near an agreement for Palestinian self-rule. *Yasir Arafat* represented the PLO in talks. That fall

Israel and Palestine signed an agreement in Washington, D.C.

By year's end, Yasir Arafat rejected the plan for self-rule. The next spring, the PLO agreed to reopen talks with Israel. An agreement was reached. Nine thousand Palestinian police were stationed in Jericho and the Gaza Strip. Israel and the PLO signed the Self-Rule Accord. Arafat and 24 others would oversee the self-rule area.

By April 1995, Palestinian suicide bombers were again active. They killed Israeli soldiers and a U.S. student in the Gaza Strip. The following month Israel agreed not to seize 134 acres of Arab land in Jerusalem. Israel and the PLO came to a new peace agreement.

In November Israel's prime minister *Rabin* was assassinated. He was shot by a citizen of Israel who thought Rabin was not hard enough on the PLO.

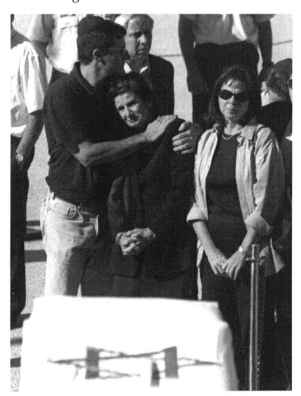

The family of Prime Minister Rabin at his funeral

Arafat was elected president of the Palestine Authority in January 1996. Two months later, there were more suicide bombing attacks on Israel. Then, in April, Palestine dropped their vow to destroy Israel. Perhaps peace had a chance.

The next January Israel agreed to leave the city of Hebron. Even so, by summer Palestine and Israel were again angry with one another. But in the fall of 1998, another sign of hope arrived. Israel's prime minister *Benjamin Netanyahu* and Arafat signed an agreement to get the peace process moving again. Netanyahu's successor also pledged to work on the peace process.

At the end of the century, peace between Israel and Palestine is not guaranteed.

Progress is made. Violence breaks out. The world can only hope there is more progress than there is violence.

Iran held local elections in 1999. Over 70 percent of those elected were in favor of reform. For the first time in many years, it looked as though Iranians might gain more personal freedom. It was possible that Iran and the U.S. might one day be more friendly to each other.

A major loss to the Middle East came in 1999. *King Hussein* of *Jordan* died. Jordan is a small nation. It borders Syria, Iraq, Saudi Arabia, and Israel. However, King Hussein helped keep peace in the region. His death caused concern about future stability in Jordan and the rest of the Middle East.

King Hussein of Jordan

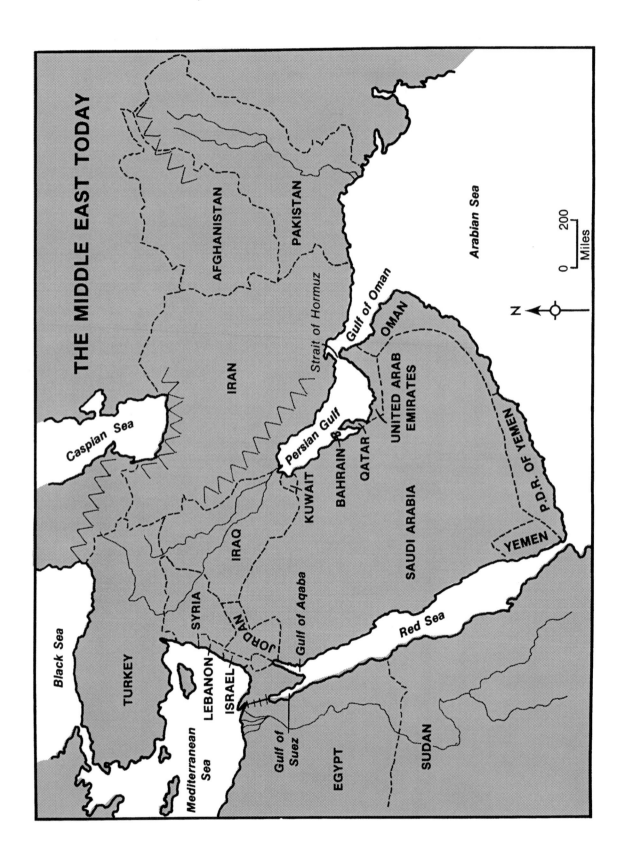

THE MIDDLE EAST TODAY

Black Sea

Caspian Sea

Arabian Sea

0   200
Miles

N

*Mediterranean
Sea*

TURKEY

AFGHANISTAN

PAKISTAN

Strait of Hormuz

IRAN

Gulf of Oman

OMAN

UNITED ARAB
EMIRATES

Persian Gulf

KUWAIT

BAHRAIN

QATAR

P.D.R. OF YEMEN

SAUDI ARABIA

YEMEN

IRAQ

SYRIA

LEBANON

ISRAEL

JORDAN

Gulf of Aqaba

Red Sea

*Gulf of
Suez*

EGYPT

SUDAN

Looking at the Map of the Middle East

Underline the location in parentheses that best completes each statement.

1. The nation of (Syria, Iraq) borders both Turkey and Iran.

2. Syria borders both (Lebanon, Saudi Arabia) and Jordan.

3. The (Red Sea, Arabian Sea) is between Sudan and Saudi Arabia.

4. The Strait of Hormuz joins the Gulf of Oman with the (Arabian Sea, Persian Gulf).

5. The Gulf of Aqaba leads to (Jordan, Lebanon).

6. (Iraq, Lebanon) borders the Mediterranean Sea.

7. Kuwait borders Saudi Arabia and (Iran, Iraq).

8. Oman and Qatar both border (Yemen, Saudi Arabia).

9. Egypt borders the Mediterranean Sea and the (Arabian Sea, Red Sea).

10. Israel shares borders with (Jordan, Iraq) and Lebanon.

Keys to the Future

Science and technology hold many of the keys to the future. Despite all our advances, we still face many problems. Cooperation and understanding must go hand in hand with science and technology.

During the summer of 1992, the UN held an *Earth Summit* in Rio de Janeiro, Brazil. Representatives from over 150 nations discussed *global warming* and the protection of the world's plants and animals.

Later that same year, 87 nations met in Denmark. They agreed to phase out *chloro-fluorocarbons* by 1996 in an effort to help save the *ozone layer.*

Another meeting of nations was held in 1997. At that time, most of the major nations banned the use of *land mines.* The United States refused to sign that agreement.

The 1990's saw great advances in the treatment of AIDS. New drugs and combinations of drugs are in use. Many people who are *HIV-positive* are slow to move on to the deadly AIDS stage of the disease. Some HIV-positive people may never have AIDS.

By the end of the century, great advances were made in *cancer* detection, prevention, and treatment. Cancer is really many different diseases. So, no one treatment is good for all cancers. There are drugs and treatments that slow the advance of some cancers. Some forms of cancer can now be cured.

On another front in medicine, some germs and diseases have *mutated,* or changed. Just as doctors find a way to kill the germs, they change to a new form. Because of mutation, some diseases have become resistant to *antibiotics.* Part of this is because doctors and patients use more antibiotics than necessary. Another factor is that some patients do not follow directions and use antibiotics incor-

rectly. Farmers who use antibiotics to increase animal and plant growth may add to the problem.

Tuberculosis is one of those diseases. Once, it was almost gone from the United States. In the 1990's, it began to reappear. Worse, some of the many types of TB can no longer be cured by most of our antibiotics.

It takes years of research for drug firms to develop new antibiotics. As more kinds of germs resist antibiotics, finding antibiotics to fight them becomes harder.

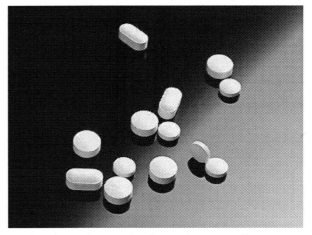

Perhaps just as bad are the new diseases that appear. *Ebola* threatened parts of Africa in the 1990's. This terrible disease caused internal bleeding until the patient died.

Diseases in animals as well as in humans have made the headlines. In 1996, *mad cow disease* was found in Great Britain. This disease causes cattle to lose control of their muscles. It comes when parts of the brain are destroyed. Mad cow disease was spread from chickens. Feed made with chicken scraps and waste gave the disease to cattle. The disease spread to people who ate undercooked meat. The rest of Europe banned British beef because of the disease.

Some scientific advances raise questions as well as give answers. The use of *DNA* to identify people has become important in fighting crime. It seems possible that DNA samples will one day be taken when a baby is born. This DNA, along with fingerprints, will be a way to positively identify that child for the rest of its life. A few people object to this form of lifetime identification.

Cloning is another advance that may help farmers. Cells from an adult animal are used to create more animals exactly like the adult. Champion animals can be reproduced. Critics fear cloning will be used in an effort to create copies of human beings.

Technology had its own problems. The Russian space station *Mir* was in orbit during the 1990's. U.S. astronauts spent time on the station as the two nations worked together. *Mir* was supposed to be the start of a new space age.

By 1997, *Mir* was showing its age. It was damaged when a spacecraft hit it during docking. This started a series of problems. *Mir's* oxygen supplies were damaged. There was a fire aboard. Electric power went out. The computer failed. For a time, it seemed the astronauts aboard were in real danger.

In May 1998, the last U.S. astronaut ever to visit *Mir* came home. The orbiting space station was to be abandoned in favor of an up-to-date international space station.

We depend on *communication satellites* in space. These satellites allow rapid communication around the world. Just how vital these satellites are was seen in 1998. One satellite developed problems. Eighty percent of the pagers in the U.S. did not work for a day or two. Doctors could not be called to emergencies. Volunteer fire and rescue units were out of touch.

We might call the 1990's the decade of *computers*. Nearly every part of our lives depends on computers. Stores use them to keep inventory. Medical records are on

computers. Airline reservations depend upon them. Our financial records are computerized. Utilities and communication services depend upon them. The list is endless.

Ever since computer *networks* were formed, *hackers* have broken into them. Many hackers are young computer users who want to see how far they can go. A few hackers deliberately cause trouble.

Hackers can invade your privacy in many ways. A hacker can change your financial records. Some have even stolen money electronically. Medical records in hospitals can be read and altered. Legal records can be changed. A person's identity can be stolen.

It is no wonder military leaders worry about hackers. The possible harm to a nation's defense is hard to imagine if hackers change computer programs or steal military information.

We depend upon computers for our safety and very lives. When air control computers go down, air traffic becomes tangled. If an air controller loses contact with the planes on his or her computer even for a few seconds, the results may be tragic.

Science and technology can do only so much. We have to use them wisely.

Think About It:

The Internet and World Wide Web have enabled you to sit in your classroom or at home and contact people all over the world. You can access information which was once found only in libraries. You have the world at the tips of your fingers.

Quick Quiz

Decide whether each statement is true or false. Write either **"T"** or **"F"** in the space before each statement to indicate your answer.

_____   1. The Camp David Accords were signed by Israel and Egypt.

_____   2. Saddam Hussein ruled Iran.

_____   3. Iraq invaded Kuwait.

_____   4. President Bush helped form the coalition that defeated Iraq.

_____   5. Yasir Arafat was elected president of Israel.

_____   6. Chlorofluorocarbons may damage the ozone layer.

_____   7. The Rio Earth Summit discussed global warming.

_____   8. Mad cow disease began in the United States.

_____   9. In 1997, the United States signed the treaty outlawing land mines.

_____   10. No new AIDS-HIV medicines have been discovered since 1985.

_____   11. Many germs now resist antibiotics.

_____   12. Computer hackers break into computer networks.

ANSWERS

Maps Help Us Understand World History

A Quick Review, page 4

1. true
2. false
3. true
4. false
5. false
6. true
7. false
8. true
9. true
10. false

The First Civilized People

Review Exercise, page 8

1. 3
2. 3
3. 2
4. 1
5. 2
6. 3
7. 3
8. 3
9. 3
10. 1
11. 2
12. 3
13. 3
14. 2
15. 3

Map Questions, page 14

1. Atlantic, Indian, Pacific, Arctic
2. Indian
3. Pacific
4. Arctic
5. a. Asia
   b. Europe
   c. Mediterranean Sea
   d. Asia
   e. Europe

Cradles of Civilization Questions, page 15

1. Sumer
2. Nile
3. Asia
4. Europe
5. Hwang Ho
6. north
7. Hwang Ho
8. Indus
9. Hwang Ho
10. 800
11. 1,600
12. 600

Puzzle Quiz, pages 17–18

Across

3. irrigation
5. alphabet
8. iron
10. barter
13. Sumer
14. laws
15. write
16. Hindus
18. caste
21. Indus
22. pyramid
23. Persia
25. tomb
26. Cyrus
27. Confucius
28. math

Down

1. Tigris
2. Yangtze
4. Nile
6. pharaoh
7. tablets
9. mummies
11. religion
12. Buddha
17. cuneiform
19. ancestor
20. Egypt
22. papyrus
24. arches

Greece and Rome

Puzzle Quiz, page 21

1. Crete
2. Sparta
3. Socrates
4. Macedonia
5. Athens

6. Philip
7. Alexander
8. Olympic
9. Golden Age
10. Greece

Ancient Greece, pages 22, 24

1. Sea of Marmara
2. Adriatic Sea
3. Bosporus
4. Hellespont
5. Persia
6. Olympia
7. Peloponnesus
8. Crete
9. Italian
10. Aegean Sea

```
E  S  A  S  E  T  E  Q  U  I  A  O
S  E  N  W  R  H  E  S  T  O  N  P
W  A  D  R  I  A  T  I  C  S  E  A
R  O  T  D  I  E  C  B  K  T  R  D
T  F  N  R  T  G  A  C  W  A  S  S
F  M  O  I  A  E  O  A  L  P  U  E
W  A  P  I  T  A  L  I  A  N  R  U
B  R  S  E  C  N  Y  T  E  O  R  O
C  M  E  S  I  S  M  A  T  A  P  O
N  A  L  T  A  E  P  E  E  I  S  A
I  A  E  A  N  C  A  I  C  R  B  U
A  T  H  U  S  T  T  E  E  B  P  R
T  P  E  R  S  I  A  N  P  O  S  O
P  E  L  O  P  O  N  N  E  S  U  S
```

Alexander the Great, pages 24–25

1. Greece, Athens, Sparta
2. Black Sea, Persia
3. Caspian Sea, Persian Gulf
4. Tigris and Euphrates, Asia
5. Nile, Egypt
6. three, Europe, Asia, Africa
7. Caucasus

Roman Empire Puzzle Quiz, page 29

Across

1. Atlantic
4. Africa
8. Nile
10. Great Britain
13. Empire
15. Mediterranean Sea
16. Strait of Gibraltar

Down

1. Apennines
2. Athens
3. Carthage
4. Alps
5. Rome
6. Adriatic

7. Asia Minor
9. Crete
11. Europe
12. Black Sea
14. Rhine

Review Exercise, page 33

1. Latin
2. Julius Caesar
3. Carthage
4. Christianity
5. Vandals

6. Senate
7. tribune
8. gladiator
9. slaves

```
L  J  U  L  I  U  S  C  A  E  S  A  R
A  P  A  O  E  S  T  R  I  B  U  N  E
T  O  D  S  C  E  D  S  L  A  V  E  S
I  P  G  V  A  N  D  A  L  S  U  S  N
N  E  B  G  L  A  D  I  A  T  O  R  S
C  H  R  I  S  T  I  A  N  I  T  Y  T
F  A  R  A  I  E  G  A  H  T  R  A  C
```

The Middle Ages

A Short Review, page 37

1. false
2. false
3. false
4. true
5. true
6. true
7. true
8. true
9. false
10. true

Puzzle Quiz, page 39

1. Islam
2. Aztec
3. Inca
4. Moors
5. Byzantine
6. Mongols
7. Koran
8. Shinto

CIVILIZATIONS

The Middle Ages, pages 44–45

Cities:
1. Constantinople
2. Rome
3. Jerusalem

Empires:
1. Muslim
2. Byzantine

Religions:
1. Eastern Orthodox
2. Islam
3. Roman Catholicism

Continents:
1. Europe
2. Europe, Asia
3. Europe, Asia, Africa

Crusades:
1. Constantinople
2. Jerusalem
3. Roman Catholicism

Later Middle Ages

True-False Puzzle, page 54

1. true
2. true
3. true
4. false
5. false
6. true
7. false
8. false
9. true
10. false
11. false

REFORMATION

Puzzle Quiz, pages 55–56

Across

2. Middle Ages
3. Aquinas
6. da Vinci
8. Parliament
12. Hanseatic
13. guild
14. Turks
17. charter
18. merchants
19. toll
21. friars
22. seaports
23. Mongols

Down

1. feudalism
2. middle class
3. apprentice
4. Ferdinand
5. universities
7. Conqueror
9. League
10. Taj Mahal
11. spices
15. Saxons
16. banking
17. Carta
20. zero

Europe's Power Grows Greater

European Colonies in the New World, pages 59, 62

1. South America and North America
2. Atlantic Ocean
3. Europe
4. Spain
5. Spain
6. Portugal
7. Spain
8. France
9. England
10. Greenland

Russia Questions, page 66

1. Moscow
2. Ivan IV
3. Catherine the Great
4. 1796
5. Baikal
6. Vladivostok
7. Baltic Sea
8. Arctic Ocean
9. Aral Sea
10. Catherine the Great

Puzzle Quiz, page 67

1. Prussia
2. Marco Polo
3. Vikings
4. despot
5. divine right
6. czar
7. Armada
8. Francisco Pizarro
9. Ferdinand Magellan
10. civil war

American Revolutionary War Puzzle Quiz, pages 71–72

Across

1. Canada
4. Savannah
6. Long
8. New Orleans
11. Ohio
14. Chesapeake Bay
15. Cape Cod
19. Gulf of Mexico
20. Savannah
21. Massachusetts
22. Valley Forge
23. Rhode
24. Mississippi River

Down

1. Cape Hatteras
2. Atlantic
3. Delaware
4. Spain
5. New York
7. Potomac
9. Erie
10. Superior
12. Ontario
13. Niagara Falls
16. Quebec
17. Delaware Bay
18. Virginia

Review Exercise, page 74

1. Pizarro
2. Marco Polo
3. Simón Bolívar
4. Hernando Cortés
5. Otto von Bismarck
6. George III
7. Congress of Vienna
8. Frederick the Great
9. czars
10. armadas

The Industrial Revolution

Industrial Britain, pages 76–77

1. Bristol
2. Manchester
3. Bristol
4. Liverpool
5. Glasgow
6. London
7. Glasgow
8. Newcastle
9. Newcastle
10. London

Puzzle Quiz, pages 80–81

Across

1. Industrial Revolution
4. Great Britain
6. raw materials
7. transportation
8. canals
11. power
12. steam engine
13. locomotives
14. invested
15. capital
16. fuel
17. factory system
18. manufacture

Down

1. inventions
2. labor
3. hand labor
5. machines
8. corporation
9. capitalism
10. markets
11. produce

Puzzle Quiz, page 85

1. capital
2. invest
3. produce
4. housing
5. socialism
6. trade
7. mercantilism
8. inventions
9. capitalism
10. locomotive
11. market
12. employer
13. river
14. corporation
15. labor force
16. fuel
17. steam engine
18. *laissez-faire*
19. communism
20. union

Puzzle Quiz, pages 86–87

1. transportation
2. communication
3. domestic system
4. population
5. socialism
6. industry
7. profits
8. labor unions
9. wages
10. *laissez-faire*
11. Karl Marx
12. employer
13. revolution
14. working conditions
15. living conditions
16. communism
17. cities
18. mercantilism
19. factories
20. freedom of contract

INDUSTRIAL REVOLUTION

The Beginning of Modern World Problems 8

Puzzle Quiz, page 91

1. imperialism
2. mother country
3. China
4. Spain
5. Germany
6. national pride
7. overpopulated
8. Hong Kong
9. Japan
10. India

Africa in 1914, pages 92–93

1. 7
2. Mediterranean Sea
3. Asia
4. French
5. British
6. French
7. French
8. Spaniards
9. in the north
10. Sahara
11. Liberia and Ethiopia
12. Nile
13. Congo

Europe in 1914, pages 96–97

1. France, Great Britain, Russia
2. Germany, Italy, Austria-Hungary
3. Rumania, Bulgaria, Greece, Albania, Montenegro
4. Italy
5. Bulgaria
6. Ottoman Empire
7. neutral
8. Great Britain
9. North Sea, Baltic Sea
10. Great Britain
11. They were located in the center of Europe.
12. Russia

Review Exercise, page 100

1. The English fought a war with China.
2. Japan fought China.
3. The Triple Entente was formed.
4. Germany became part of the Triple Alliance.
5. The European arms race began.
6. Trenches were dug on the Western Front.
7. The *Lusitania* was sunk.
8. An armistice was signed between the Allies and Germany.
9. Lenin led the Russian people to revolt against the government.
10. Germany was unified.

The World in the Twentieth Century 9

Europe, 1919–1929, Between World War I and World War II; pages 102–103

1. Finland
2. Russia
3. Soviet Union
4. Estonia, Latvia, and Lithuania
5. Russia
6. Poland
7. Germany, Russia

8. Czechoslovakia, Yugoslavia
9. Rumania was smaller in 1914 than it was in 1929.
10. Yugoslavia
11. Russia

Puzzle Quiz, page 107

1. Lenin
2. Stalin
3. Roosevelt
4. Nazi
5. Mussolini
6. Franco
7. Hitler
8. Fascist
9. Siberia
10. Ruhr
11. Commonwealth
12. dictator

```
C R M O R B T
O O U C A D H
M S S N D I N
M E S A D C U
O V O R S T A
N L F T A I
W E I N A T R
E N A L T E
A T I Z I R B
L E N I N H I
T S T E I U S
H I T L E R J
F A S C I S T
```

Puzzle Quiz, page 111

Across

1. Chiang Kai-shek
5. Soviet Union
6. Rhineland
9. Pearl Harbor
10. Allies
11. Japan
12. Lend-Lease

Down

1. Churchill
2. Axis
3. blitzkrieg
4. Hiroshima
7. Eisenhower
8. Gandhi
10. atomic

Review Exercise, page 115
I. b, a, c, e, d   III. c, b, a, e, d
II. a, e, b, c, d   IV. d, b, e, c, a

Puzzle Quiz, page 116
1. North Korea
2. South Korea
3. Rhee
4. elections
5. MacArthur
6. United Nations
7. Korean War
8. Japan
9. truce

Years of Hope and Disappointment 10

Modern Map of the Middle East, page 120
1. a peninsula
2. Turkey
3. Jordan
4. Dead Sea
5. Red Sea
6. Its territory got larger.
7. Egypt
8. Jordan
9. Israel
10. Gulf of Aqaba
11. Mediterranean Sea
12. Red Sea
13. Egypt
14. Lebanon
15. Jordan River

Puzzle Quiz, page 122
Across
4. Mideast
7. Israel
8. Arafat
10. Elath
12. Six-Day
14. Syria
15. OPEC
18. Palestinian
19. Lebanon
21. barrel
22. Muslims

Down
1. import
2. Nasser
3. Sadat
5. embargo
6. Suez
9. Arab
11. hostages
13. hijack
16. PLO
17. civil
20. oil

Postwar Europe Puzzle Quiz, pages 128–129
Across
1. Soviet Union
4. Belgium
6. Rumania
7. Yugoslavia
9. Norway
13. Czechoslovakia
15. Austria
17. France
18. Great Britain
23. Baltic Sea
25. Netherlands
27. Finland
28. Spain
29. Greece

Down
1. Sweden
2. Turkey
3. Italy
4. Bulgaria
5. Mediterranean
8. Albania
10. Denmark
11. North
12. Portugal
14. East Germany
16. Switzerland
19. Black Sea
20. Ireland
21. Poland
22. Germany
24. Atlantic
26. Hungary

Puzzle Quiz, pages 130–131
1. cold war
2. Florida
3. Ho Chi Minh
4. Mao Tse-tung
5. communism
6. Nixon
7. exiles
8. East
9. missile
10. Eisenhower
11. Castro
12. Berlin
13. Budapest
14. Kissinger
15. Hungary
16. revolt
17. Kennedy
18. Paris
19. Taiwan
20. China
21. Tonkin
22. Indochina

Puzzle Quiz, pages 130–131 (continued)

23. dictator
24. Vietnam
25. Cambodia
26. Johnson
27. curtain
28. Warsaw
29. Stalin
30. Cuba
31. Yugoslavia

A Time of Change and Progress

Asia in 1980, page 134

1. Atlantic
2. Soviet Union
3. Korea
4. Malaysia and Indonesia
5. Bhutan
6. Mongolia
7. Taiwan and Sri Lanka
8. Soviet Union
9. Cambodia
10. four

Puzzle Quiz, page 138

1. Gandhi
2. Benelux
3. France
4. North Sea
5. Northern Ireland
6. NATO
7. Franco
8. Pakistan
9. guerrilla
10. Steel
11. Irish
12. Hindu
13. Indira
14. Common Market
15. petroleum
16. civilians
17. Bangladesh
18. Spain
19. Protestant
20. trade

Puzzle Quiz, pages 140–141

1. orbit
2. satellite
3. astronaut
4. Laika
5. Glenn
6. *Mariner*
7. *Eagle*
8. *Sputnik*
9. *Tiros*
10. Gagarin
11. *Telstar*
12. Shepard
13. *Salyut*
14. *Explorer*
15. *Apollo*
16. *Luna*
17. *Echo*
18. *Gemini*

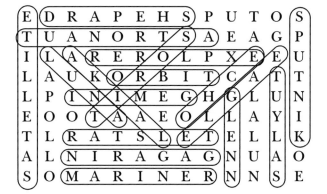

Puzzle Quiz, pages 145–146

1. Zimbabwe
2. Ghana
3. Rhodesia
4. Ethiopia
5. export
6. rebels
7. independent
8. apartheid
9. Selassie
10. mutiny
11. Portugal
12. Angola
13. famine
14. Transkei
15. income
16. civil
17. Somalia
18. colony
19. Bantu
20. Mozambique
21. Italy
22. Belgium
23. copper
24. parliament
25. Smith

A Quick Review, page 149

1. Zimbabwe, Zambia
2. France
3. population
4. Mugabe
5. South Africa
6. locusts
7. emergency
8. Mandela

Checking Up, page 153

1. Ride
2. Chernobyl
3. toxic
4. Clark
5. ozone
6. greenhouse
7. *Columbia*
8. viruses
9. AIDS
10. artificial

Toward the Twenty-first Century

Compare Turn of the Century Europe with Post War Europe, page 165

1. East and West Germany have united.
2. Czechoslovakia divided into the nations of the Czech Republic and Slovakia.
3. Belarus, Ukraine, Estonia, Latvia, Lithuania, Moldova
4. Slovenia, Croatia, Bosnia and Herzegovina, Yugoslavia, Macedonia

Looking Back, page 170

1. L
2. L
3. E
4. E
5. L
6. A
7. E
8. L
9. A
10. A
11. E
12. A
13. E
14. A
15. E
16. E

Looking at the Map of the Middle East, page 177

1. Iraq
2. Lebanon
3. Red Sea
4. Persian Gulf
5. Jordan
6. Lebanon
7. Iraq
8. Saudi Arabia
9. Red Sea
10. Jordan

Quick Quiz, page 180

1. T
2. F
3. T
4. T
5. F
6. T
7. T
8. F
9. F
10. F
11. T
12. T

GLOSSARY

acid rain—rain with a high acid content, which harms plants and buildings

Acquired Immune Deficiency Syndrome (AIDS)—a disease that destroys the body's ability to fight infection

Aldrin, Edwin—U.S. astronaut, one of the first people to land on the moon

Alexander the Great—king of Macedonia who conquered lands from Greece to India

Alfred the Great—king of England

Allies—World War I: Great Britain, France, and Russia

alphabet—set of letters used for writing where each letter stands for a sound

American Revolution—war of 1776 in which the American colonies became independent from Britain

Angles—Germanic tribe that invaded England in the fifth century

Antarctic Circle—line of latitude 66° south of the equator

antibiotics—drugs used to combat infections

apartheid—strict segregation policy once applied in South Africa

apprentice—beginning worker

aqueduct—structure made to bring water from one area to another

Aquino, Corazon—prime minister of the Philippines

Arabic numerals—system of numbers that we use today, developed in India and brought to Europe by Arabs

Arafat, Yasir—leader of the PLO

architecture—the art of designing buildings

Arctic Circle—line of latitude 66° north of the equator

Aristotle—ancient Greek philosopher, student of Plato

armistice—agreement to stop fighting

Armstrong, Neil—U.S. astronaut, one of the first people to land on the moon

Assyria—ancient empire in the near east, in the area where Iraq is today

astronomy—study of the stars

Athens—ancient Greek city-state where idea of democracy began

Augustus—ruler of ancient Rome

Austria-Hungary—central European kingdom that included what is now Austria, Hungary, Slovenia, Croatia, and northeastern Italy

Axis powers—World War II alliance between Germany, Italy, and Japan

Aztec—early empire in the area that is Mexico today

Babylonia—ancient country in the valley between the Euphrates and Tigris rivers, near where Iraq is today

Balkan Peninsula—a peninsula in southeastern Europe, containing Slovenia, Croatia, Bosnia and Herzegovina, Macedonia, Yugoslavia, Romania, Bulgaria, Albania, Greece, and part of Turkey

barter—to trade one thing for another without using money

Batista, Fulgencio—Cuban dictator defeated in 1959 by Fidel Castro

Bay of Pigs—1961 invasion of Cuba, supported by the U.S. government

Begin, Menachem—prime minister of Israel

Belgian Congo—former name of the Democratic Republic of Congo

Benelux—trading group made up of Belgium, the Netherlands, and Luxembourg

benevolent despot—ruler who has complete power, but largely works for the good of the people

Berlin Airlift—system of delivering supplies to Berlin when Soviets closed off roads to the city

Berlin Wall—barrier built by the Soviets to separate East Berlin, which was under Communist rule, from West Berlin, which was controlled by western powers

Bhutto, Benazir—prime minister of Pakistan

Bible—holy book of Christianity

Bismarck, Otto von—Prussian leader who helped form a united Germany

Blair, Tony—prime minister of the United Kingdom

Bolívar, Simón—South American liberator

Bonaparte, Napoleon—French emperor

Bourbons—royal family of France

Boxer Rebellion—1900 attempt to throw foreigners out of China

Buddhism—religion based on the teachings of the Buddha

Bush, George—U.S. president

Byzantine Empire—Eastern Roman empire, centered on the city of Constantinople (today called Istanbul)

capital—wealth that is used to produce more wealth

capitalism—economic system in which factories, farms, and other properties are privately owned

caravel—Portuguese three-masted sailing ship

Carthage—city in North Africa, destroyed by Rome

caste—hereditary social class system in Hinduism

Castro, Fidel—Communist dictator of Cuba

Catherine the Great—empress of Russia

Central Powers—World War I alliance between Germany and Austria-Hungary

Charlemagne—leader of the Franks

charter—a paper given to a city by a nobleman, stating that the people of the town were free

Chechyna—province of Russia

Chernobyl—Russian nuclear generating plant that released large amounts of radiation, exposing thousands of people

chivalry—the customs and rules followed by knights

chlorofluorocarbons (CFC's)—gasses, once used in air conditioners and refrigerators, that harm the ozone layer

Christianity—religion based on the teachings of Christ

Churchill, Winston—British prime minister during World War II

city-state—a state that is made up of a city and the land around it

civil war—a war between citizens of the same country

civilian—a person who is not in the armed forces

Clinton, Bill—U.S. president

cold war—rivalry and mistrust that stops short of actual fighting

Columbus, Christopher—explorer who introduced Europe to the Americas in 1492

Common Market—European trading group that led to the European Union

Commonwealth of Nations—association of self-governing nations that had been part of the British Empire

communism—social system where factories, farms, and other property are owned by everyone in common

computer virus—computer program designed to damage computer hardware and software

Confucianism—system of ethics based on teachings of Confucius

Confucius—Chinese teacher and thinker who lived about 2,500 years ago

Congress of Vienna—meeting of European leaders after defeat of Napoleon

conquer—to beat, defeat

Constantinople—the center of the Byzantine Empire; the city called Istanbul today

constitution—the basic laws and principles that govern a country

consul—in ancient Rome, a chief magistrate, elected to the position every year

copper—easily worked reddish metal

corporation—an organized group of people running a business

Cortés, Hernando—Spanish soldier who invaded and conquered Aztec empire in Mexico in 1519

Crete—island in the Mediterranean where an early civilization developed

Crusade—a military expedition that European Christians made in the eleventh, twelfth, and thirteenth centuries to capture Jerusalem from the Muslims

Cyrus the Great—ruler of ancient Persia

Czechoslovakia—former name for Czech Republic and Slovakia

da Gama, Vasco—explorer who sailed around Africa in 1497

da Vinci, Leonardo— Renaissance artist

Dark Ages—period in European history after the end of the Roman Empire

Declaration of Independence—paper stating that the American colonies were a free nation

democracy—government in which the people have a say in who their rulers are

Deng Xiaoping—Chinese leader

depression—a period where businesses go down and many people are unemployed

despot—ruler

dhow—small sailboat used by Arab sailors

drought—a period where little or no rain falls

dynasty—a succession of rulers in the same family

Eisenhower, Dwight—U.S. general who led Allied army in Europe during World War II; U.S. president

embargo—government order stopping trade with a country

emperor—ruler of an empire

empire—a group of nations headed by a single ruler

equator—an imaginary line that runs from east to west around the center of the earth

Euphrates—river in Asia where earliest civilizations began

euro—currency of the European Union

European Coal and Steel Community—trading group in Europe that led to the European Union

European Union—trading group in Europe

factory system—system of producing things in factories instead of in workers' homes

Falkland Islands—islands in the Atlantic Ocean invaded by Argentina in 1982

famine—extreme lack of food

Fascist party—Italian political party

Ferdinand of Castile—king who, with his wife Isabelle, united Spain

fertile—good for growing crops

feudalism—political and economic system in Europe during the Middle Ages, where a lord granted land and protection to people who gave the lord services and part of their crops in return

Ford, Gerry—U.S. president

Formosa—old name for Taiwan

Francis Ferdinand—Austrian archduke whose assassination sparked off World War I

Franco, Francisco—Spanish dictator

Franks—people who settled the area known as France today

Frederick the Great—king of Prussia

freedom of contract—system where each worker met with the employer to set wages

French Indochina—French colony in Southeast Asia, now Laos, Cambodia, and Vietnam

French Revolution—1789 revolution that destroyed the French king and nobles

Gadhafi, Muammar—leader of Libya

Gagarin, Yuri—Soviet cosmonaut, first person to orbit earth

Gandhi, Indira—Indian prime minister

Gandhi, Mohandas "Mahatma"—Indian leader whose policy of passive resistance helped India gain independence from Britain

Gandhi, Rajiv—prime minister of India

Gaul—Roman province, where France is today

Genghis Khan—Mongol leader

geometry—branch of mathematics that deals with lines and angles

George III—king of England at the time of the American Revolution

Ghana—West African empire, about A.D. 700

gladiator—professional fighter of ancient Rome

Glenn, John—U.S. astronaut

globe—model of the earth

Golden Age of Greece—period in ancient Greece where philosophy, building, and the arts flourished

Gorbachev, Mikhail—Soviet leader at the time of the collapse of the Soviet Union

government—a system for running a country

Great Wall of China—fifteen-hundred-mile long wall built to protect China from invaders

greenhouse effect—an increase in the temperature of the earth caused by emissions trapped in the atmosphere

guerrilla—unofficial soldier who uses sudden raids and ambushes, not outright battles

guild—medieval organization, resembling today's labor union

Gulf of Tonkin—1964 incident in which it was claimed that U.S. ships had been fired on by North Vietnam

Hammurabi—king of Babylon who set up a written system of laws

Hanseatic League—medieval organization that helped merchants trade between countries

Hapsburgs—royal family of Spain and Austria

Havel, Václav—Czech writer, president

hieroglyphics—form of writing used in ancient Egypt where pictures stood for sounds and words

Hindu—Indian religion

Hitler, Adolf—German leader before and during World War II

Ho Chi Minh—leader of the Vietnamese uprising against France, president of North Vietnam

Holocaust—the mass slaughter of civilians, especially Jews, during World War II

Holy Roman Empire—a loose organization of German and Italian territories

homeland—an area set aside by the South African government for black residents only

Huang Ho—river in China where an early civilization developed

Hussein, Saddam—leader of Iraq

illiteracy—being unable to read

imperialism—adding new colonies to make an empire bigger

Inca Empire—early empire in the area that is Peru today

Indus River—river in what is now Pakistan where an early civilization developed

Industrial Revolution—rapid change in the economy as machines were developed and the way things were manufactured changed

Irish Republican Army (IRA)—terrorist organization in Northern Ireland

iron curtain—political barrier that separated Communist Europe from the rest of Europe

irrigation—bringing water to fields in order to grow crops

Isabelle of Aragon—queen who, with her husband Ferdinand, united Spain

Islam—religion based on the teachings of Muhammad

Joan of Arc—Frenchwoman who helped defeat an English army

Julius Caesar—Roman general and ruler

Jutes— Germanic tribe that invaded England in the fifth century

Chiang Kai-shek—Chinese Nationalist leader

Kennedy, John. F.—U.S. president

Khomeini, Ayatollah—leader of Iran after the shah was overthrown

Kissinger, Henry—U.S. government official

knight—a soldier in the Middle Ages who served a king or lord

Korean War—(1950–1953) war fought in Korea between North Koreans and South Koreans, supported by United Nations troops

Kublai Khan—Mongol leader, grandson of Genghis Khan

Kurds—ethnic group living in Turkey and Iraq

labor union—an organization of workers formed to protect the workers' interests

laissez-faire—system where the government does not interfere in business and trade

Latin—the language of ancient Rome

latitude, lines of—lines drawn one degree apart on maps and globes that are parallel to the equator

law—a rule to regulate the way people act

League of Nations—an association of nations formed after World War I to promote world peace

Lenin, Vladimir—leader of Russian revolution

Livingstone, David—English explorer in Africa

locust—a grasshopper that travels in a large swarm, often doing great damage to crops

longitude, lines of—lines drawn one degree apart on maps and globes that run from the North Pole to the South Pole

Lusitania—ship sunk in 1915 by German submarine, killing 1,198 passengers

Luther, Martin—German monk whose objections to certain Church practices helped bring about the Reformation

MacArthur, Douglas—U.S. general who led American forces in Asia

Magellan, Ferdinand—explorer whose ships sailed around the world between 1519 and 1522

Magna Carta—document that English barons forced their king to sign; it gave the English people certain rights

Mali—West African empire, about A.D. 1100

Manchuria—Asian country invaded by Japan in 1931

Mandela, Nelson—leader of the ANC, imprisoned for 27 years by the white government, who became the first black prime minister of South Africa

mansa—ruler of Mali

Mao Tse-tung—communist leader of China

map—a flat picture of the earth, or a part of it

Marco Polo—Italian merchant who spent years in China and wrote a book about his travels

Marx, Karl—German thinker who developed Marxism

Mecca—city in Arabia; holy city of Islam, to which Muslims make a pilgrimage

Meir, Golda—prime minister of Israel

mercantilism—economic system where the government controlled business and trade

merchant—a person who buys and sells goods

Mesopotamia—region between the Tigris and Euphrates rivers where several early civilizations began

Michelangelo—Renaissance artist

Middle Ages—the period of European history from about A.D. 500 to about 1500

middle class—class of people, between the rich and the poor, that developed during the Middle Ages

monastery—a place where a group of monks live and work

Mongols—a northern Asian tribe who invaded China

monk—a man who belongs to a religious order and promises to follow its rules

Montezuma—ruler of the Aztecs at the time of the Spanish invasion

Moors—Muslims who conquered Spain

Mubarak, Hosni—president of Egypt

Muhammad—prophet of Islam

mummy—the body of a person that has been preserved from decay after death

Muslim—follower of Islam

Mussolini, Benito—Italian Fascist premier before and during World War II

mutiny—rebellion against authority by soldiers or sailors

Nasser, Gamal—leader of Egypt

National Socialist party—Nazi party

Nazi party—party that controlled Germany from 1933 to 1945 under Adolf Hitler

Netanyahu, Benjamin—prime minister of Israel

neutral—not taking sides in a disagreement or war

New Deal—programs developed to end the Depression in the U.S.

Nightingale, Florence—Englishwoman whose work improved conditions in hospitals

Nile—long river in Africa that flows through Egypt to the Mediterranean

Nixon, Richard M.—first U.S. president to visit China

Nok—early civilization where Nigeria is today

Noriega, Manuel—dictator of Panama, captured by U.S. forces in a 1990 invasion

North Atlantic Treaty Organization (NATO)—agreement among nations that they would help each other in the event of a Soviet attack

North Pole—the most northern point on the earth

OPEC (Organization of Petroleum Exporting Countries)—trade group of countries that export oil

orbit—the path taken by one body as it revolves around another

overpopulation—when more people live in an area than the area can support

ozone layer—part of the atmosphere that protects us from the damaging rays of the sun

Pakistan—Muslim nation created in 1947 when India gained independence from Britain

Palestine Liberation Organizatio (PLO)—group fighting for a Palestinian homeland

papyrus—early form of paper, made from reeds

parallel of latitude—see latitude

Parliament—the lawmaking body of the United Kingdom

Pearl Harbor—port in Hawaii where Japanese bombers destroyed the U.S. navy in 1941

peasant—poor farmer

People's Republic of China—name adopted by China in 1949

Pericles—ruler of ancient Greece

Perry, Matthew—American sailor who opened Japan to trade with the west

Persia—early civilization in the area where Saudi Arabia is today

Peter the Great—czar of Russia

pharaoh—ruler of ancient Egypt

philosopher—a thinker, someone who seeks wisdom

Phoenicia—early civilization in the area where Syria is today

physical features—mountains, rivers, deserts, lakes, etc.

Pizarro, Francisco—Spanish soldier who conquered the Incas

Plato—ancient Greek philosopher, student of Socrates

political map—map that shows national borders; often uses color or shading to tell nations and regions apart

pollution—human-made waste that dirties the air or water

pope—leader of the Catholic Church

population density—how close people live to each other in an area

precipitation—rainfall

Prime Meridian—line of longitude that runs from the North Pole to the South Pole through Greenwich, England; used as the starting point for measuring east and west around the globe

prime minister—the head of the government

profit—the amount of money left after all the costs are taken away from income

propaganda—information carefully chosen to spread an idea

Protestant—a Christian belonging to a church that broke away from the Roman Catholic Church

province—in ancient Rome, a country or region brought under Roman control

Prussia—German state, north of Austria

pyramids—huge stone tombs built by rulers of ancient Egypt

Rabin, Yitzhak—prime minister of Israel

Raphael— Renaissance artist

Reagan, Ronald—U.S. president

Reformation—a sixteenth century religious movement to change some practices of the Roman Catholic Church; it led to the development of the Protestant churches.

religion—belief in and worship of a god or gods

Renaissance—a period in Europe between the fourteenth and seventeenth centuries when there was much activity in the arts and science

republic—a type of government elected by the people

revolution—a complete change in government or rule

Rhodesia—former name of Zimbabwe and Zambia

Ride, Sally—first female U.S. astronaut

Rome—city in Italy; center of an ancient civilization

Roosevelt, Franklin D.—U.S. president whose programs helped end the Depression in the U.S.

Ruhr Valley—part of Germany where coal mines and steel mills were located

Russian Revolution—1917 revolution that overthrew the Russian ruling family, set up a communist government

Sadat, Anwar—president of Egypt

Sahara Desert—North African desert

samurai—Japanese warrior

San Martin, Jose de—South American soldier and statesman

satellite—an object or vehicle made to orbit the earth

Saxons— Germanic tribe that invated England in the fifth century

scale of distance—a line on a map that shows how much of earth's surface each part of the map stands for

segregation—policy of keeping white and nonwhite people separate

Selassie, Haile—emperor of Ethiopia

Senate—body of lawmakers

serf—in feudalism, someone who was completely subject to the will of a lord

Shephard, Alan B.—U.S. astronaut

Shi Huangdi—first emperor of China

Shinto—Japanese religion

shogun—Japanese military leader

Siberia—northeastern part of Russia where people who disagreed with government policy were sent

Smith, Ian—prime minister of Rhodesia

social security—government pension program

socialism—social system where certain businesses are controlled by the government

Socrates—ancient Greek philosopher

solar power—method of generating heat and electricity by using the sun

Songhai—West African empire, about A.D. 1450

South Pole—the most southern point on earth

Soviet Union—U.S.S.R.

Spanish Armada—great fleet of ships built to attack England

Sparta—warlike ancient Greek city-state

Stalin, Joseph—harsh Russian leader who made the country into a police state

Suez Canal—canal that leads from the Mediterranean to the Red Sea

Sumer—early civilization in the area where Iraq is today

Taiwan—island off the coast of China where Nationalist Chinese moved after Chinese Revolution

Taj Mahal—beautiful tomb in India, built by a king for his dead wife

Telstar—communications satellite

Tenochtitlan—capital of the Aztec empire, now called Mexico City

Thatcher, Margaret—(1925–1987) first woman prime minister of the United Kingdom

Tiananmen Square—large square in Beijing, China, where student protests were crushed in 1989

Tigris—river in Asia where earliest civilizations began

Titian—Renaissance artist

Tito—dictator of Yugoslavia

tournament—medieval contest in which knights tried to unhorse each other

trade—the business of buying and selling goods

Treaty of Versailles—meeting of leaders to agree on peace terms after World War I

trench—a long narrow ditch used to protect soldiers in battle

trench warfare—warfare where soldiers attack from trenches facing each other

Triple Alliance—pre-World War I alliance between Germany, Austria-Hungary, and Italy

Triple Entente—pre-World War I alliance between Great Britain, France, and Russia

Truman, Harry S.—U.S. president who ordered dropping atomic bombs on Hiroshima and Nagasaki

Tudors—royal family of England

unemployment insurance—program where employers pay into a fund so that people who lose their jobs have an income while they look for work

Union of Soviet Socialist Republics (U.S.S.R.)—name taken in 1922 by Russia and states under Russian rule

Vandals—Germanic tribe who overran Gaul, Spain, northern Africa, and Rome

vassal—a person who was protected by a lord in return for supporting the lord

Victoria—(1819–1901) English queen whose long rule gave the name to an era

Visigoths—Germanic tribe who overran the Roman Empire

Walesa, Lech—leader of the Polish Solidarity movement, prime minister, winner of the Nobel Peace Prize

Waterloo—place where Napoleon's armies were defeated by the English and Germans

William the Conqueror—Frenchman who defeated the English and became the first king of a united England

Wilson, Woodrow—U.S. president who proposed forming a League of Nations after World War I

workers' compensation—insurance program to pay doctor expenses if a worker is hurt on the job

Yeltsin, Boris—president of Russia after the collapse of the Soviet Union

Zaire—former name of the Democratic Republic of Congo